The British Army of George II, 1727–1760

Gabriele Esposito is a military historian who works as a freelance author and researcher for some of the most important publishing houses in the military history sector. In particular, he is an expert specializing in uniformology: his interests and expertise range from the ancient civilizations to modern post-colonial conflicts. During recent years, he has conducted and published several researches on the military history of the Latin American countries, with special attention on the War of the Triple Alliance and the War of the Pacific. He is among the leading experts on the military history of the Italian Wars of Unification and the Spanish Carlist Wars. His books and essays are published on a regular basis by Osprey Publishing, Winged Hussar Publishing and Libreria Editrice Goriziana. He is also the author of numerous military history articles appearing in specialized magazines such as *Ancient Warfare Magazine*, *Medieval Warfare Magazine*, *The Armourer*, *History of War*, *Guerres et Histoire*, *Focus Storia* and *Focus Storia Wars*.

The British Army of George II, 1727–1760

History, Organization and Equipment

Gabriele Esposito

Pen & Sword
MILITARY

First published in Great Britain in 2024 by
Pen & Sword Military
An imprint of
Pen & Sword Books Limited
Yorkshire – Philadelphia

ISBN 978 1 39905 190 3

A CIP catalogue record for this book is
available from the British Library

Typeset by Mac Style
Printed and bound in India by Replika Press Pvt. Ltd.

Pen & Sword Books Limited incorporates the imprints of After the Battle,
Atlas, Archaeology, Aviation, Discovery, Family History, Fiction, History,
Maritime, Military, Military Classics, Politics, Select, Transport, True Crime,
Air World, Frontline Publishing, Leo Cooper, Remember When, Seaforth
Publishing, The Praetorian Press, Wharncliffe Local History, Wharncliffe
Transport, Wharncliffe True Crime and White Owl.

For a complete list of Pen & Sword titles please contact

PEN & SWORD BOOKS LIMITED
47 Church Street, Barnsley, South Yorkshire, S70 2AS, England
E-mail: enquiries@pen-and-sword.co.uk
Website: www.pen-and-sword.co.uk
or
PEN AND SWORD BOOKS
1950 Lawrence Rd, Havertown, PA 19083, USA
E-mail: uspen-and-sword@casematepublishers.com
Website: www.penandswordbooks.com

MIX
Paper from
responsible sources
FSC® C016779

Contents

Acknowledgements

This book is dedicated to my parents, Maria Rosaria and Benedetto, for the immense love and great support that they have given me throughout my life. A very special thanks goes to Philip Sidnell, the commissioning editor of my books for Pen & Sword: his love for military history and his passion for publishing are fundamental for the success of our publications. A special mention goes to the production manager of this title, Matt Jones, for his hard work and great competence. Many thanks also to Tony Walton, for his precious editing and for his friendship. Most of the pictures published in this book are in the public domain, obtained from the magnificent Digital Collections of the New York Public Library and Digital Repository of the Brown University Library. Everyone with an interest in military history can easily browse the vast contents of these at https://digitalcollections.nypl.org/ and https://repository.library.brown.edu/studio/.

Introduction

The main aim of this book is to provide a detailed overview of the history, organization and uniforms of British military forces during the long reign of George II (1727–1760). This period was an extremely important one in the history of Great Britain, since it saw the emergence of what gradually became the British Empire. When George II ascended to the throne in 1727, the British Army was relatively small, having been demobilized after the glorious days of the War of the Spanish Succession (1701–1714). This long-running conflict had seen British forces, guided by the brilliant Duke of Marlborough, obtaining a series of astonishing victories on the battlefields of mainland Europe (something that had not happened since the late Middle Ages). Marlborough forged the British Army and transformed it into one of the best military forces in Europe, introducing high standards of discipline and new tactics. It should also be noted that it was during the crucial years of the War of the Spanish Succession that the English Army and the Scottish Army were finally assembled together in order to create a unified British Army; as we will see in the first chapter of this book, by the outbreak of the Glorious Revolution in 1688 there had been three regular armies in the British Isles (all autonomous from each other): the English Army, the Scottish Army and the Irish Army. During the period 1727–1760, British military forces were greatly expanded and participated in two major international conflicts in continental Europe and beyond: the War of the Austrian Succession (1740–1748) and the Seven Years' War (1756–1763). British participation in these wars was not particularly brilliant on the European front, where they suffered some significant defeats and achieved no great victories; but in the rest of the world, on the colonial fronts, the situation was completely different. By 1760, thanks to the successes obtained during the early phase of the Seven Years' War, Great Britain had been able to expel the French from both Canada and India. This, from many points of view, was a pivotal moment in the long history of the British Empire.

In this book, we will detail the history, organization and uniforms of the various components of the British military during the period 1727–1760. In the first chapter, we will provide an overview of the military situation in the British Isles as it was before the creation of the British Army. Chapter 2 will deal with the guard infantry units, while the third chapter will focus on the line infantry, including the Corps of Invalids and the Fencible Corps. The fourth and fifth chapters will analyze the Highland infantry and the light infantry. Chapter 6 will cover the guard cavalry units, with Chapter 7 dedicated to the heavy cavalry (horse and dragoon regiments) and Chapter 8 to the light cavalry. The ninth chapter will analyze the technical corps of the Royal Artillery and Royal Engineers, as well as the naval infantry, and the tenth chapter will cover the auxiliary corps created to face the Jacobite Uprising of 1745 and the allied contingents from Germany and the Netherlands that fought for Britain during the period 1745–1760. The eleventh chapter will be dedicated to the colonial forces deployed in the Thirteen Colonies of North America and in the West Indies of the Caribbean, with extensive details of the American militia and provincial military units. Chapter 12 will cover the military contingents of the East India Company, and the last chapter will provide a general overview of the uniforms and equipment employed by all the military units described in the previous chapters of this book.

Chapter 1

The Birth of the British Army

When James II became king in 1685, the English Army was in a state of neglect. The days of glory of the New Model Army had long been forgotten, the fighting force of 65,000 veterans forged by Cromwell having been reduced to just 8,800 men. In early 1686, the English Army comprised the following units:

- The Royal Regiment of Guards
- The King's Footguards (also known as the Coldstream Guards)
- The Royal Regiment of Foot, with twenty line companies and one of grenadiers
- The Queen Dowager's Regiment of Foot, with ten line companies and one of grenadiers
- Prince George of Denmark's Regiment of Foot, with twelve line companies and one of grenadiers
- The Holland Regiment of Foot, with twelve line companies and one of grenadiers
- The Queen Consort's Regiment of Foot, with ten line companies and one of grenadiers
- The Life Guards, with three troops of guardsmen and three companies of horse grenadiers
- The King's Regiment of Horse, with eight troops
- The Royal Regiment of Dragoons, with six troops
- Twenty-four independent line infantry companies

The Royal Regiment of Guards, later known as the 1st Foot Guards, were created in 1665 by merging two infantry regiments that already had 'guard' status and duties: Lord Wentworth's Regiment of Foot and John Russell's Regiment of Foot. The first had been raised in 1656 by the future Charles II during his exile in the Spanish Netherlands and initially consisted of professional soldiers who were loyal to the Stuarts. With the Restoration of 1660, the unit came to England and became part of the reorganized English Army. John Russell's Regiment was created in 1660 after Charles II's return to England; it mirrored the functions and structure of Lord Wentworth's

Regiment and soon became a duplicate of it. In 1665, it was decided to assemble the two guard regiments into a single unit, which received the new denomination of the Royal Regiment of Guards. The King's Footguards had been raised in 1650 as one of the infantry regiments that made up Cromwell's New Model Army. Initially known as Monck's Regiment of Foot, in 1660 it supported the Restoration of the Stuarts and made an epic march of five weeks from Coldstream (in Berwickshire) to London in order to side with Charles II. Due to this episode, it soon received the nickname of 'Coldstream Guards' from the name of the village where the elite infantrymen had started their march. In 1661, the unit received the new official denomination of the Lord General's Regiment of Foot Guards, which was later changed to the King's Footguards. Despite being older than the Royal Regiment of Guards, it was always placed as the second most senior regiment of the English infantry because it had entered royal service only in 1660 (until then it had been part of the New Model Army and not of the royal forces). The Royal Regiment of Guards had twenty-six companies divided into two battalions, with thirteen companies in each; the King's Footguards had a single battalion with thirteen companies. One company in each battalion was made up of grenadiers, while the other twelve consisted of mixed pikemen (one-third of the soldiers) and musketeers (two-thirds of the soldiers). Each company consisted of one captain, one lieutenant, one ensign, two sergeants, three corporals, two drummers and eighty privates. The regimental staff comprised one adjutant, one quartermaster/provost marshal, one chaplain, one surgeon and one drum-major. Line infantry companies, be they from a regiment or independent ones scattered across England with garrison duties, all had the same internal composition: one captain, one lieutenant, one ensign, two sergeants, three corporals, one drummer and sixty privates. Grenadier companies carried no colours, and thus their officers consisted of one captain and two lieutenants but they had three sergeants instead of two. One-third of the privates in each line company were armed with pikes, the rest being equipped with muskets, while grenadier companies and independent line infantry companies were entirely made up of musketeers.

The 1st Troop of Lifeguards was raised in 1658 as part of the military forces organized by Charles II during his exile in the Spanish Netherlands. The 2nd Troop was raised in the same year, being named The Duke of York's Troop of Horse Guards' and the 3rd Troop was created in 1659 as Monck's Lifeguards (being the mounted bodyguard of George Monck, the main political supporter of Charles II). Members of the Lifeguards were known as 'gentlemen', as they all came from the higher social classes of the country and were required to provide their own horse and uniform. The companies of horse grenadiers, which were attached to each troop of 'gentlemen' since 1678, were made up of ordinary soldiers. The internal composition of a troop was as follows: one captain, four lieutenants, one cornet, one guidon, one quartermaster, four brigadiers, four sub-brigadiers, four trumpeters, one kettledrummer and 200 'gentlemen'. The companies of horse grenadiers had two lieutenants, two sergeants, two corporals, two drummers, four hautboys (an archaic form of oboe) and sixty-four privates. In 1686, the 4th Troop of Lifeguards was raised, with its own company of horse grenadiers. The King's Regiment of Horse was the only heavy cavalry unit of the English Army in 1685; each of its troops comprising the following elements: one captain, one lieutenant, one cornet, one quartermaster, three corporals, two trumpeters and fifty troopers. The senior troop also comprised a small regimental staff made up of one adjutant, one chaplain, one surgeon, one quartermaster and one kettledrummer. The Royal Regiment of Dragoons, like all the dragoon units of the European armies in the late seventeenth century, was a mounted infantry corps and not a proper cavalry unit: its members were trained to move on horse but to fight on foot. The regiment was created from veteran cavalrymen who had served in the short-lived English colony of Tangier until 1683, and each of its troops consisted of the following elements: one captain, one lieutenant, one cornet, one quartermaster, two sergeants, three corporals, two drummers, two hautboys and fifty dragoons. The senior troop also comprised one adjutant, one quartermaster, one chaplain, one surgeon and one gunsmith. A few months after becoming king, James II decided to expand the English Army in a significant way, ordering the creation of the following new units (which took place between 1686 and 1688):

- The Royal Regiment of Fuzileers
- Princess Anne of Denmark's Regiment of Foot, with ten line companies
- Henry Cornwall's Regiment of Foot, with twelve line companies and one of grenadiers
- The Earl of Bath's Regiment of Foot, with twelve companies
- The Duke of Beaufort's Regiment of Foot, with ten line companies
- The Duke of Norfolk's Regiment of Foot, with ten line companies
- The Earl of Huntingdon's Regiment of Foot, with ten line companies
- Sir Edward Hales' Regiment of Foot, with ten line companies
- Sir William Clifton's Regiment of Foot, with ten line companies
- The Queen's Regiment of Horse, with nine troops
- The Earl of Peterborough's Regiment of Horse, with six troops
- The Earl of Plymouth's Regiment of Horse, with six troops
- The Earl of Thanet's Regiment of Horse, with six troops
- The Earl of Scarsdale's Regiment of Horse, with six troops
- Baron Lumley's Regiment of Horse, with six troops

- Princess Anne's Regiment of Dragoons, with eight troops
- The Queen's Regiment of Dragoons, with six troops

The Royal Regiment of Fuzileers was organized from the outset as an elite unit, being made up of twelve line companies (entirely equipped with muskets) and a single company of miners. The latter were uniformed and equipped like standard grenadiers, but also carried hammer-hatchets and thus acted as combat engineers. The Royal Regiment of Fuzileers was created to act as the escort for the Train of Artillery. In the late seventeenth century, artillerymen were required to fire their guns but were not equipped to defend themselves from enemy attacks. As a result, while on the battlefield they had to be escorted by a unit of infantrymen specifically charged to do so. It should be noted that until 1716, with the formation of the Royal Artillery, the English Army did not comprise any permanent company/battery of artillery: temporary artillery trains were organized by the Ordnance Department only when needed, and were usually disbanded at the end of each campaign. In times of peace, around 225 professional gunners were at the service of the Ordnance Department, scattered across England and manning the guns of the various garrisons. In case of war, they were assembled to form an artillery train and were supplemented with the required number of civilian mattrosses and pioneers, the latter being semi-skilled civilian labourers who were contracted only for the duration of a campaign. The conductors of the carts that were used to move the artillery pieces were also all civilians. In the summer of 1686, six infantry regiments (of which only four were English) were each given two brass 3-pdr guns, which were to be used as battalion guns. James II wanted to attach some artillery to his infantry regiments, as happened in most European armies of the time. This experiment was not a complete success, especially because no gunners were added to the regiments and the pieces thus had to be manned by line infantrymen. Consequently, no other regiments received the battalion guns.

During the summer of 1685, as part of his military reforms, James II rationalized the organization of his infantry by ordering the absorption of seven of the independent infantry companies into the line regiments. At the same time, the number of troops in the Royal Regiment of Dragoons was expanded to twelve and Princess Anne's Regiment of Dragoons was raised. Some time later, the Royal Regiment of Dragoons was reduced to eight troops and Princess Anne's Regiment of Dragoons to six, in order to create the new Queen's Regiment of Dragoons with six troops. In July 1685, it was ordered that all regiments of horse were to have a uniform establishment with six troops; only The King's Regiment of Horse and The Queen's Regiment of Horse were permitted to have a higher establishment, with nine troops. During February/March 1686, all the remaining independent companies of infantry were transformed into grenadier units and were attached to the newly raised regiments of foot (most of which did not have a grenadier company). Thanks to the transformation of the garrison companies, it was also possible to add two more line companies to The Queen Dowager's Regiment of Foot and The Queen Consort's Regiment of Foot. A few weeks before the outbreak of the Glorious Revolution, James II ordered that each infantry regiment was to have a standard establishment of twelve line companies and one grenadier company. The Royal Regiment of Foot was increased to a total of twenty-six companies, assembled into two battalions, each with thirteen companies. On 17 January 1688, James II also ordered the recall of all the English and Scottish soldiers who were serving in the Dutch Army as part of the veteran Anglo-Scots Brigade. This unit had been created in 1586 by assembling together all the English and Scottish military units that were supporting the Netherlands in its war of liberation against Spain. It consisted from the beginning of six regiments, three recruited from English professional soldiers and three from Scottish ones. In 1664, shortly before the outbreak of the Second Anglo-Dutch War, the three English regiments went back to their homeland, but in 1675 they returned to the Netherlands to be reincorporated into the Anglo-Scots Brigade. In 1688, William of Orange, at that time ruler of the Netherlands and claimant to the English throne, refused to permit the transfer of the entire Anglo-Scots Brigade to England, but could not prevent some of its members from going back home. These, once in England, were organized into three new units: John Hales' Regiment of Foot (assigned to the English Army), John Wachop's Regiment of Foot (assigned to the Scots Army) and Roger McElligott's Regiment of Foot (assigned to the Irish Army). The original regiments of the Anglo-Scots Brigade later followed William of Orange during his invasion of England that took place as part of the Glorious Revolution, and remained on English pay until the end of the Grand Alliance War (1688–1697). In 1697, one of the English regiments was disbanded and the other two were made part of the English Army; the three Scottish regiments, instead, returned to the Netherlands, where they continued to form a Scots Brigade until 1795. In 1688, when William of Orange's invasion of England was imminent, James II ordered the raising of another seven infantry regiments: these, however, could not be properly trained and equipped by the time William landed in England. During this last expansion of his infantry, James II also ordered the raising of thirty-one new independent companies in order to free the regular regiments from their garrison duties. Two of these new units were recruited from Pensioners of the Royal Hospital, who were no longer fit for active service but who could still be employed as static troops. Six new regiments of horse were raised shortly before William of Orange's landing, but like their infantry equivalents they had not been properly trained and equipped when the invasion took place.

After the Restoration of 1660, the Privy Council of Scotland established a small standing army that was completely autonomous from the English Army and was primarily tasked with keeping order among the Highland communities. This comprised the following units in 1685, when James II became King of Scotland:

- The Scots Regiment of Foot Guards
- The Royal Scots Fuzileers
- The Lifeguards
- The Royal Regiment of Scots Horse
- The Royal Regiment of Scots Dragoons

As in the English Army, no permanent Scottish artillery units existed. The Scots Regiment of Foot Guards, created as early as 1642, became a guard unit during 1650 and soon started to be considered as the best corps of the Scottish Army. In early 1685 it comprised a total of eleven companies, ten of which were of line infantry and one of grenadiers. Soon after James II's coronation, however, the establishment of the regiment was expanded with the addition of another four line infantry companies. During 1686, the unit, despite being a Scottish one, was transferred to the establishment of the English Army. The internal composition of its companies and of its regimental staff was exactly the same as the English guard regiments, except for the additional presence of one piper and four hautboys in the staff. The Royal Scots Fuzileers were raised in 1678 and were initially equipped with pikes and muskets, like the English regiments of foot. Around 1680, however, the unit became a fusilier regiment because all its members were given muskets. The corps had an establishment of ten line infantry companies and one grenadier company; another line infantry company was added to the regiment in 1685. Both the Scots Regiment of Foot Guards and the Royal Scots Fuzileers always followed the organizational changes that were introduced by James II for the English Army. The monarch, however, did not expand his Scottish troops as he did with the English ones: only one new infantry regiment was added to the Scottish Army before the Glorious Revolution. This was John Wachop's Regiment of Foot, which was raised from Scottish soldiers of the Anglo-Scots Brigade who returned to their homeland.

The single troop of Scots Lifeguards did not have an attached company of horse grenadiers like the troops of English Lifeguards. Its internal composition was as follows: one captain, two lieutenants, one cornet, one guidon, one quartermaster, four brigadiers, four trumpeters, one kettledrummer, one surgeon, one assistant-surgeon, one clerk, one farrier and 118 guardsmen. The unit was quartered in Edinburgh and was to act as the mounted bodyguard of the king when he was in Scotland. The

Royal Regiment of Horse comprised six troops and its internal structure was exactly the same of its English equivalent; during James II's reign, the unit followed all the organizational changes that were introduced for the English cavalry. It had originally been formed in 1678 as three independent companies, which were augmented to four and assembled into a regiment in late 1682. The last two troops were added in 1684. The Royal Regiment of Dragoons, later known as the Scots Greys from the colour of its first uniform (not initially from the colour of its mounts), was created in 1678 as three independent troops of dragoons. These were augmented to six troops and assembled into a regiment during 1681. The internal composition of the companies was the same as their English equivalents and the unit followed all the organizational changes that were introduced for the English dragoons during James II's reign. Like the English Army, the Scottish Army also included a number of professional gunners and independent infantry companies having garrison duties. Finally, there were also twelve Independent Highland Companies charged with countering cattle rustling and with keeping order in the Highlands. The small Scottish Army, later expanded by William of Orange, continued to exist as an independent military force until 1707, when its units were absorbed into the new British Army.

Like the English and Scottish armies, the Irish Army was completely reformed after the Restoration of 1660. During Charles II's reign (1660–1685), it was greatly expanded by the king, since the Catholic Irishmen were his most loyal subjects. In 1685, the Irish Army comprised the following units:

- The Irish Regiment of Foot Guards
- The Duke of Ormonde's Regiment of Foot
- The Earl of Granard's Regiment of Foot
- The Viscount of Mountjoy's Regiment of Foot
- Sir Thomas Newcommen's Regiment of Foot
- Sir William King's Regiment of Foot
- Hamilton's Regiment of Foot
- Fairfaix's Regiment of Foot
- The Lifeguards
- The Duke of Ormonde's Regiment of Horse
- The Earl of Arran's Regiment of Horse
- The Earl of Ossory's Regiment of Horse

The Irish Regiment of Foot Guards was raised in 1662 and initially comprised 1,200 men in twelve companies, originally being mostly made up of Protestants, all veterans of Cromwell's New Model Army. Since 1685, however, all Protestant officers of the unit had been rapidly replaced by James II, and by the outbreak of the Glorious Revolution the whole unit was comprised of Catholics. In 1685, the regiment had twelve companies of line infantry and one of grenadiers. The internal composition of the companies and of the regimental staff was exactly the same as the English guard regiments, except for the additional presence of one piper in the staff. When Charles II reorganized the Irish Army following his Restoration, all the existing regular units were assembled into a large corps known as the Royal Regiment of Ireland, which consisted of eight independent companies of infantry and twenty independent troops of cavalry. Later, in 1684, another reorganization took place: the existing units, supplemented with some veteran companies from Tangier, were expanded to form seven regiments of infantry and three regiments of cavalry. The infantry units all had twelve companies of line infantry and one company of grenadiers, while the regimental staff consisted of the following elements: one adjutant, one quartermaster, one chaplain, one surgeon and one assistant surgeon. During James II's reign, the Irish regiments of foot always had the same internal composition as their English equivalents and followed the organizational changes introduced for them. Only one new infantry unit was added to the Irish Army before the Glorious Revolution: Roger McElligott's Regiment of Foot, which was raised from Irish soldiers of the Anglo-Scots Brigade who returned to their homeland. The single troop of Irish Lifeguards had an attached company of horse grenadiers like the troops of English Lifeguards, and had the same internal composition. The unit was quartered in Dublin and acted as the mounted bodyguard of the king when he was in Ireland. The three regiments of horse had an establishment of eight troops each, and from 1684 onwards each of them had an attached company of dragoons. The internal structure of the Irish cavalry regiments was the same as their English equivalents (except for the fact that each troop had forty-five horsemen and one trumpeter), and during James II's reign all the organizational changes introduced for the English horse units were followed. The companies of dragoons had the same internal structure as the horse troops. During the autumn of 1685, two more troops were added to each Irish cavalry regiment. At the same time, the companies of dragoons were absorbed into a new regiment that had been raised in England and that was later transferred to the Irish Army. This was Hamilton's Regiment of Dragoons, which was the first independent unit of dragoons to be formed in Ireland and which had a large establishment with ten troops. Shortly before William of Orange's invasion, James II ordered the creation of four new Irish units (three regiments of infantry and one of dragoons), but these were not raised in time to fight in England. Following the end of the Glorious Revolution, the Irish Army ceased to be a fully autonomous military institution, being transformed into the Irish Establishment of the English Army, which became part of the British Army in 1707.

Chapter 2

Guard Infantry

All the European armies of the early eighteenth century included a number of guard units, which made up an elite inside the military of each country. These could be small bodyguard corps, having as their main function escorting the monarch, or larger combatant units with superior training and morale. In Great Britain, the Royal Guard had a very long tradition, consisting of combat units with a special status and performing peculiar duties. In 1727, the infantry component of the British Royal Guard comprised three regiments: 1st Foot Guards, 2nd Foot Guards (or Coldstream Guards) and 3rd Foot Guards (or Scots Guards). Each of these three infantry units had a very particular history, from which the nicknames of the corps came. The 1st Foot Guard was created in 1665 through the merger of two infantry regiments that already had guard status and duties: Lord Wentworth's Regiment and John Russell's Regiment. The first had been raised in 1656 by the future Charles II during his exile in the Spanish Netherlands (present-day Belgium), initially consisting of professional soldiers who had followed the future monarch into exile and were loyal to the Stuarts. With the Restoration in 1660, the unit came back to England and became part of the reorganized English Army. John Russell's Regiment was created in 1660, after Charles II's return to England; it mirrored the functions and structure of Lord Wentworth's Regiment and soon became a duplicate of it. In 1665, it was decided to unite the two guard regiments into a single unit, which received the new denomination of the 1st Regiment of Foot Guards. The 2nd Foot Guards was created in 1650, as one of the infantry regiments that made up Cromwell's New Model Army. Initially known as Monck's Regiment of Foot, in 1660 it supported the Restoration of the Stuarts and made an epic march of five weeks from Coldstream (in Berwickshire, southern Scotland) to London in order to support Charles II. It soon received the nickname of the Coldstream Guards from the village where the elite infantrymen had started their march. After the Restoration, the regiment remained in London to keep order in the capital. In 1661, due to its loyalty towards Charles II, it received the new official denomination of The Lord General's Regiment of Foot Guards. Although the 2nd Foot Guards was older than the 1st Foot Guards, it was placed as the second most senior regiment of the Household Troops because it had entered royal service after the 1st Foot Guards (until 1661, it had formally been part of the New Model Army and not of the royal forces). To underline the fact that their corps was older than the 1st Foot Guards, members of the Coldstream Guards adopted as their regimental motto the phrase '*Nulli Secundus*' ('second to none'). In 1670, the unit adopted its definitive denomination of the Coldstream Regiment of Foot Guards. The 3rd Foot Guards was the oldest of the three guard regiments, but it was the last to enter English royal service; as a result, it was placed as the third most senior unit of the Household Troops. The regiment was created in 1642 as part of the Scottish Army, not the English one; until 1707, the Scotland's military remained independent from that of England since the nations were two autonomous kingdoms. Charles I, as King of Scotland, ordered the formation of what was to become the 3rd Foot Guards in order to face the Irish rebellion of 1641. The unit was raised by the Marquess of Argyll, Archibald Campbell, thus having as its first denomination the Marquis of Argyll's Royal Regiment. In 1650, when Charles II became King of Scotland following the execution of his father, the unit became guard regiment and adopted the new title of the Lyfe Guard of Foot. In 1651, following Cromwell's victories over the supporters of Charles II, the Scottish Guards were disbanded, being reformed ten years later when Charles II assumed the English and Scottish thrones. Now known as the Scottish Regiment of Foot Guards, it was later transferred (1686) to the establishment of the English Army and thus became part of the English Royal Guard, albeit being a Scottish corps. In 1712, after England and Scotland had been united into a single state in 1707, the Scots Guards were given their final denomination of the 3rd Regiment of Foot Guards.

In 1727, the three regiments of foot guards had two battalions each, being larger than most of the British line infantry regiments, which consisted of only a single battalion. In 1760, a third battalion was added to the 1st Regiment, this being the only significant organizational change that took place during the period 1727–1760. As was the case with the line infantry units, each battalion consisted of nine line companies (musketeers) and one grenadier company (heavy infantry). Grenadiers emerged as a new troop type of European infantry during the second half of the seventeenth century, when the various armies started to employ hand-grenades as a new weapon. These could be thrown by infantrymen and were quite simple to produce. They were of great use during siege operations and could also be employed during pitched battles to destroy enemy field fortifications. In order to use the new weapon most effectively, the various infantry units of the European armies started to select their tallest and strongest men to be retrained as grenadiers and learn how to use hand-grenades on the battlefield. The French Army was the first to create independent sub-units of grenadiers within its infantry regiments, a company of grenadiers being included in each infantry battalion in 1671. During the following decades, grenadiers quickly became the elite of the French foot troops, thanks to their superior training and discipline. As time progressed, the French innovations were also adopted by the other European armies, and grenadiers could be found practically everywhere in the Continent. Many monarchs later transformed their units of grenadiers into elite corps with guard status, and this new category of heavy

The uniforms of the 1st Foot Guards, from left to right: officer, drummer, non-commissioned officer (NCO), fifer, grenadier and musketeer. This plate, like several others reproduced in the following pages, is part of Richard Knotel's *Uniformenkunde*.

infantry became increasingly popular. In addition to the standard ten companies, some British foot regiments could have one or two additional companies in wartime; these, which never left the homeland, were not intended to go on active service but instead to function as recruit depots. In case of military emergency, as happened during the Jacobite Uprising of 1745, the additional companies of different regiments could be assembled together in order to form temporary provisional battalions. On campaign, furthermore, the grenadier companies of different infantry regiments could be detached from their parent units to create temporary grenadier battalions. Being ad hoc corps made up of elite soldiers, these were usually employed to perform special missions.

Each British infantry battalion had three field officers: a colonel, lieutenant colonel and major. The colonel was the commander of the unit and was responsible for its recruitment; each regiment of foot could be considered as the private property of its commanding colonel. This was reflected in the denomination of the various units, which were named after their colonel until progressive numbering was introduced in 1742. The only exception to this rule was those regiments – usually the oldest ones of the British Army – which had peculiar denominations comprising the adjective 'Royal'. The lieutenant colonel was the second in command and could replace the colonel on most occasions, whereas the major was particularly responsible for training and discipline in his battalion (assisted in his functions by an adjutant). Each of the companies was commanded by a captain, except for the senior company that had a captain lieutenant (who ranked as his regiment's senior lieutenant). The captain of each line infantry company was assisted by a lieutenant and an ensign; the captain of a grenadier company, instead, was assisted by a lieutenant and a second lieutenant. Each infantry battalion had a small staff consisting of the following elements: an adjutant (usually a meritorious NCO who had been promoted from the ranks), quartermaster (tasked with a series of important administrative functions), surgeon and chaplain. In theory, each infantry company was to comprise eighty men, and thus a battalion was to deploy 800 soldiers; in practice, however, these official establishments were usually respected only by the three regiments of foot guards and a few line infantry units. Each company mustered three sergeants, three corporals, two drummers and seventy privates; the musicians of grenadier companies were two fifers instead of drummers. The senior company of each battalion had five sergeants rather than the standard three.

The 1st Battalion of the 1st Foot Guards fought under Marlborough during the War of the Spanish Succession, earning an excellent reputation as it took part into the following engagements: Schellenberg (1704), Blenheim (1704), Ramilies (1706), Oudenarde (1708) and Malplaquet (1709). With the outbreak of the War of the

Musketeer of the 1st Foot Guards. This plate, along with numerous others reproduced in the following pages, is part of the *Cloathing Book* published in 1742 to show all the uniforms worn at that time by the British Army. The creation of the *Cloathing Book*, which was a prototype for the illustrated dress regulations later published by other European armies, was commissioned by the Duke of Cumberland, commander of the British Army at that time.

Austrian Succession in 1740, the 1st Battalion of the 1st Foot Guards was mobilized again and sent to the Continent; this time it was part of a Brigade of Guards that also included the 1st Battalion of the 2nd Foot Guards and the 3rd Foot Guards. The unit participated in the Battle of Dettingen in 1743 and Battle of Fontenoy in 1745 (the latter being the worst defeat suffered by the British Army in the War of the Austrian Succession). The grenadier companies of the three guard battalions that had remained in Great Britain were mobilized to fight against the Jacobite insurgents in Scotland. In 1758, during the Seven Years' War, the Brigade of Guards was re-formed to conduct an amphibious operation against the coastline of northern France, but this was short-lived and ended in complete failure. The 1st Battalion of the 2nd Foot Guards was involved into the War of the Spanish Succession from 1708, when it was brigaded with the 1st Battalion of the 1st Foot Guards, fighting with distinction at the Battle of Oudenarde (1708) and Battle of Malplaquet (1709). The battalion was mobilized again for the War of the Austrian Succession, during which it was part of the Brigade of Guards. After the end of the Jacobite Uprising, in 1747, a new Brigade of Guards was raised by assembling the second battalions of the three guard regiments. This brigade was sent to Flanders, but did not see any major fighting before the hostilities came to an end in 1748. The 1st Battalion of the 2nd Foot Guards was part of the short-lived Brigade of Guards created in 1758. In 1760, the second battalions of the three guard regiments were joined together in a new Brigade of Guards that was sent to Germany. This formation did not see any major fighting before the end of the Seven Years' War, except for participating (marginally) in the Battle of Wilhelmstal in 1762. During the Spanish War of Succession, the 3rd Foot Guards did not send any of its battalions to fight on the Continent under Marlborough. Between 1704 and 1714, however, the unit included a special Highland company tasked with patrolling the wild territory of northern Scotland. This independent corps, which anticipated many features of the future Independent Highland Companies, was dressed and equipped in Highland fashion. In 1710, the 2nd Battalion of the 3rd Foot Guards briefly participated in a punitive expedition conducted against the Spanish coastline. It should be remembered that the 3rd Foot Guards assumed its definitive denomination and status only in 1712, due to its Scottish origins. The 1st Battalion of the 3rd Foot Guards was mobilized for the War of the Austrian Succession, during which it was part of the Brigade of Guards that fought at Dettingen and Fontenoy. The unit was also part of the short-lived Brigade of Guards created in 1758.

As the above makes clear, the foot guard regiments of the British Army took part in several of the most important military operations conducted by Great Britain during the period 1727–1760. They were not parade bodyguard corps but proper

Musketeer of the 2nd Foot Guards.

Musketeer of the 3rd Foot Guards.

combat units, whose level of professionalism was unrivalled in Europe. The backbone of the three regiments was represented by the NCOs, professionals who were able to train their men skilfully. It was their duty to transform young recruits into battle-hardened veterans, by preserving the traditions of their regiment. Obedience, endurance, loyalty and pride were the four key factors behind the elite status of the foot guardsmen. Uniforms and equipment, for example, always had to be in perfect order and completely clean, especially when performing guard duties. Most of the common soldiers serving in the foot guard regiments came from the militia, and thus already had some experience of military life. Under the guidance of their NCOs,

The uniforms of the guard infantry's grenadiers, from left to right: grenadier of the 1st Foot Guards, grenadier of the 2nd Foot Guards and grenadier of the 3rd Foot Guards. This oil painting, like several reproduced in the following pages, is part of a series initiated in 1751 by the Anglo-Swiss military painter David Morier. This collection, part of the Royal Collection Trust, was commissioned by the Duke of Cumberland, third son of George II, a lover of uniformology in addition to being the victor of the Battle of Culloden. (*Royal Collection Trust / © His Majesty King Charles III 2024*)

however, they rapidly turned into professionals who were able to face any combat situation. Even more important than the NCOs, however, were the officers, who gave the foot guard regiments their real and distinctive character. Most officers came from aristocratic families of landowners, who had long military traditions. They were known as 'gentlemen's sons', but despite their high social status they showed on most occasions that their military competence was unrivalled and they were not lacking courage. Buying an officer's commission in the guard infantry regiments was extremely costly, meaning that only the young sons of the aristocracy could do so. Daily life, in time of peace, was very expensive for these officers: it was spent in the most prestigious gentlemen's clubs of London and they were obliged to invest large sums of money in order to have the most elegant uniforms needed to be part of high society.

Chapter 3

Line Infantry

Line infantry regiments were the most numerous component of the British Army during the eighteenth century, although despite their official denomination of 'regiments', they overwhelmingly consisted of just single battalions comprising nine companies of line infantrymen and one company of grenadiers. Only a few units, such as the famous 1st Regiment of Foot, were an exception to this general rule and consisted of two battalions instead of one. However, the two battalions of these handful of extra-large regiments always acted as independent units and were never brigaded together. Until 1742, British line infantry regiments were known by the name of their commanding colonel, but from that year each of them received a progressive number that reflected the seniority of each unit. In times of war, the number of companies in each regiment could be increased with the formation of various additional companies, which were not intended to go on active service but to function as recruiting depots. Three of each regiment's companies were commanded by the field officers of the corps: a colonel (who also commanded the entire unit), lieutenant colonel (second in command for the entire regiment) and major. The latter was a fundamental component of the unit, being responsible for the training and discipline of all the companies. The other seven companies were commanded by captains, and there also was a second captain who could replace the colonel as company commander when he was absent. Each officer commanding a company was assisted by a lieutenant and an ensign; in the grenadier company, the latter was substituted by a second lieutenant. In addition to the company officers listed above, each regiment had another four commissioned staff officers: an adjutant, quartermaster, surgeon and chaplain. The quartermaster was the most important of these, performing a series of vital practical functions like keeping order in the ranks and supervising the construction of camps and field fortifications. Each company comprised three sergeants, three corporals and two drummers, in addition to seventy privates. The grenadier companies had two fifers as musicians, while the colonel's company had five sergeants instead of three. The two additional NCOs in the regimental commander's company were a sergeant major and a quartermaster sergeant. The senior sergeant of each company also acted as pay sergeant and thus had an important administrative role. In addition to the above, each infantry company had a pioneer, who was a soldier specifically trained to act as a combat engineer. The ten pioneers of each regiment could be assembled together into a single squad and employed to build fortifications or remove any obstacle that might be encountered by their unit during a march. On campaign, most of the infantry companies had less than seventy privates each, as it was not easy to replace losses very rapidly; the only exception to this rule was the grenadier companies, the full establishment of which was always maintained. Single grenadier companies of various regiments could frequently be detached from their parent units in order to form temporary grenadier battalions, these temporary corps usually being employed to conduct special operations. Grenadiers were hand-picked veterans with great combat experience and were chosen from the tallest and strongest men of each unit. Some British infantry regiments had the peculiar denomination of 'fusiliers', which derived from the fact that their members had always been armed only with muskets when most foot regiments still comprised soldiers equipped with pikes. The fusilier regiments retained their elite status during the eighteenth century; all their members were uniformed like grenadiers and not ordinary line infantry. The following regiments of foot were part of the British infantry during the period 1727–1760:

1st Regiment of Foot, The Royal: raised in 1661 as part of the Scottish Army, it was transferred to the English Army in 1678.

2nd Regiment of Foot, The Queen's Royal: raised in 1661 to act as the garrison of Tangier in Morocco.

3rd Regiment of Foot, The Buffs: originally raised for Dutch service, it became part of the English Army in 1665.

4th Regiment of Foot, The King's Own: raised in 1680 to reinforce the garrison of Tangier in Morocco.

5th Regiment of Foot: originally raised for Dutch service, it became part of the English Army in 1685.

6th Regiment of Foot: originally raised for Dutch service, it became part of the English Army in 1685.

7th Regiment of Foot, Royal English Fusiliers: raised in 1685 as the Ordnance Regiment, it was originally tasked with escorting the artillery train.

8th Regiment of Foot, The King's: raised in 1685 as Princess Anne of Denmark's Regiment of Foot.

Musketeers of the 1st Foot (left) and the 2nd Foot (right).

Musketeers of the 3rd Foot (left) and the 4th Foot (right).

9th Regiment of Foot: raised in 1685 as Henry Cornewall's Regiment of Foot.

10th Regiment of Foot: raised in 1685 as the Earl of Bath's Regiment of Foot.

11th Regiment of Foot: raised in 1685 as the Duke of Beaufort's Regiment of Foot.

Musketeers of the 5th Foot (left) and the 6th Foot (right).

12th Regiment of Foot: raised in 1685 as the Duke of Norfolk's Regiment of Foot.

13th Regiment of Foot: raised in 1685 as the Earl of Huntingdon's Regiment of Foot.

Fusilier of the 7th Foot (left) and musketeer of the 8th Foot (right). The 7th Foot was a fusilier regiment known as the Royal English Fusiliers.

Grenadiers from various regiments, from left to right: 7th Foot, 4th Foot and 8th Foot. (*Royal Collection Trust / © His Majesty King Charles III 2024*)

14th Regiment of Foot: raised in 1685 as Sir Edward Hales' Regiment of Foot.

15th Regiment of Foot: raised in 1685 as Sir William Clifton's Regiment of Foot.

16th Regiment of Foot: raised in 1688 as Archibald Douglas' Regiment of Foot.

17th Regiment of Foot: raised in 1688 as Solomon Richard's Regiment of Foot.

18th Regiment of Foot, The Royal Irish: raised in 1684 as part of the Irish Army, it became part of the English Army in 1688.

19th Regiment of Foot: raised in 1688 as Francis Lutterell's Regiment of Foot.

20th Regiment of Foot: raised in 1688 as Sir Richard Peyton's Regiment of Foot.

21st Regiment of Foot, Royal Scottish Fusiliers: raised in 1678 as part of the Scottish Army, it became part of the English Army in 1688.

22nd Regiment of Foot: raised in 1689 as the Duke of Norfolk's Regiment of Foot.

23rd Regiment of Foot, Royal Welsh Fusiliers: raised in 1689 as Lord Herbert's Regiment of Foot.

24th Regiment of Foot: raised in 1689 as Sir Edward Dering's Regiment of Foot.

25th Regiment of Foot: raised in 1689 as the Earl of Leven's Regiment of Foot.

26th Regiment of Foot: raised in 1689 as the Earl of Angus' Regiment of Foot.

27th Regiment of Foot, Inniskilling: raised in 1689 as Zachariah Tiffin's Regiment of Foot.

28th Regiment of Foot: raised in 1694 as Sir John Gibson's Regiment of Foot, it was disbanded in 1697 and re-raised in 1702.

29th Regiment of Foot: raised in 1694 as Thomas Farrington's Regiment of Foot, it was disbanded in 1698 and re-raised in 1702.

30th Regiment of Foot: raised in 1694 as Thomas Saunderson's Regiment of Foot, it was disbanded in 1698 and re-raised in 1702.

31st Regiment of Foot: raised in 1702 as a regiment of marines, it was transformed into a line unit in 1714.

32nd Regiment of Foot: raised in 1702 as a regiment of marines, it was transformed into a line unit in 1715.

33rd Regiment of Foot: raised in 1702 as the Earl of Huntingdon's Regiment of Foot.

34th Regiment of Foot: raised in 1702 as Lord Lucas' Regiment of Foot.

35th Regiment of Foot: raised in 1701 as part of the Irish Establishment, it became part of the British Army in 1702.

36th Regiment of Foot; raised in 1701 as part of the Irish Establishment, it became part of the British Army in 1702.

37th Regiment of Foot: raised in 1702 as Thomas Meredyth's Regiment of Foot.

Musketeers of the 9th Foot (left) and the 10th Foot (right).

38th Regiment of Foot: raised in 1702 as Luke Lillingston's Regiment of Foot.

39th Regiment of Foot: raised in 1702 as Richard Coote's Regiment of Foot.

40th Regiment of Foot: raised in 1717 as Richard Philipps' Regiment of Foot.

Musketeers of the 11th Foot (left) and the 12th Foot (right).

Grenadiers from various regiments, from left to right: 10th Foot, 11th Foot and 12th Foot. (*Royal Collection Trust / © His Majesty King Charles III 2024*)

41st Regiment of Foot, Royal Invalids: raised in 1719 from the companies of the Invalid Corps.

42nd Regiment of Foot, James Oglethorpe's Regiment: raised in 1737 and disbanded in 1747.

42nd Regiment of Foot, Royal Highland: raised in 1739 from the Independent Highland Companies.

43rd Regiment of Foot, Alexander Spotswood's Regiment: raised in 1739 and disbanded in 1742.

43rd Regiment of Foot: raised in 1741 as Thomas Fowke's Regiment of Foot.

Musketeers of the 13th Foot (left) and the 14th Foot (right).

Musketeers of the 15th Foot (left) and the 16th Foot (right).

44th Regiment of Foot: raised as the 1st Regiment of Marines in 1739, disbanded in 1748.

44th Regiment of Foot: raised in 1741 as James Long's Regiment of Foot.

45th Regiment of Foot: raised as the 2nd Regiment of Marines in 1739, disbanded in 1748.

45th Regiment of Foot: raised in 1741 as Daniel Houghton's Regiment of Foot.

46th Regiment of Foot: raised as the 3rd Regiment of Marines in 1739, disbanded in 1748.

46th Regiment of Foot: raised in 1741 as John Price's Regiment of Foot.

47th Regiment of Foot: raised as the 4th Regiment of Marines in 1739, disbanded in 1748.

47th Regiment of Foot: raised in 1741 as Sir John Mordaunt's Regiment of Foot.

48th Regiment of Foot: raised as the 5th Regiment of Marines in 1739, disbanded in 1748.

48th Regiment of Foot: raised in 1741 as James Cholmondeley's Regiment of Foot.

49th Regiment of Foot: raised as the 6th Regiment of Marines in 1739, disbanded in 1748.

49th Regiment of Foot: raised in 1743 as Edward Trelawney's Regiment of Foot.

50th Regiment of Foot: raised as the 7th Regiment of Marines in 1739, disbanded in 1748.

50th Regiment of Foot, American Provincials: raised in 1754 for service in New England, disbanded in 1756.

50th Regiment of Foot: raised in 1755.

51st Regiment of Foot: raised as the 8th Regiment of Marines in 1739, disbanded in 1748.

51st Regiment of Foot, Cape Breton Regiment: raised in 1754 for service in New England, disbanded in 1756.

Musketeers of the 17th Foot (left) and the 18th Foot (right). The 18th Regiment of Foot was one of the few units to have a coat without frontal lapels.

Grenadiers from various regiments, from left to right: 17th Foot, 16th Foot and 18th Foot. (*Royal Collection Trust / © His Majesty King Charles III 2024*)

51st Regiment of Foot: raised in 1755.

52nd Regiment of Foot: raised as the 9th Regiment of Marines in 1739, disbanded in 1748.

52nd Regiment of Foot: raised in 1755.

53rd Regiment of Foot: raised as the 10th Regiment of Marines in 1740, disbanded in 1748.

53rd Regiment of Foot: raised in 1755.

54th Regiment of Foot: raised in 1755.

55th Regiment of Foot: raised in 1755.

56th Regiment of Foot: raised in 1755.

Musketeers of the 19th Foot (left) and the 20th Foot (right). The 20th Regiment of Foot was one of the few units to have a coat without frontal lapels.

Fusilier of the 21st Foot (left) and musketeer of the 22nd Foot (right). The 21st Foot was a fusilier regiment known as the Royal Scottish Fusiliers.

Fusilier of the 23rd Foot (left) and musketeer of the 24th Foot (right). The 23rd Foot was a fusilier regiment known as the Royal Welsh Fusiliers.

57th Regiment of Foot: raised in 1755.

58th Regiment of Foot: raised in 1755.

59th Regiment of Foot: raised in 1755.

60th Regiment of Foot, Royal American: raised in 1755, it was a light infantry regiment.

61st Regiment of Foot: raised in 1756.

62nd Regiment of Foot: raised in 1756.

63rd Regiment of Foot: raised in 1756.

64th Regiment of Foot: raised in 1756.

65th Regiment of Foot: raised in 1758.

66th Regiment of Foot: raised in 1758.

67th Regiment of Foot: raised in 1758.

68th Regiment of Foot: raised in 1758.

69th Regiment of Foot: raised in 1758.

70th Regiment of Foot: raised in 1758.

71st Regiment of Foot, Invalids: raised in 1758 from the Invalid Corps, disbanded in 1768.

72nd Regiment of Foot, Invalids: raised in 1758 from the Invalid Corps, disbanded in 1768.

73rd Regiment of Foot, Invalids: raised in 1762 from the Invalid Corps, disbanded in 1769.

74th Regiment of Foot, Invalids: raised in 1762 from the Invalid Corps, disbanded in 1769.

75th Regiment of Foot, Invalids: raised in 1762 from the Invalid Corps, disbanded in 1769.

76th Regiment of Foot: raised in 1758 and disbanded in 1763.

77th Regiment of Foot, Montgomerie's Highlanders: raised in 1758 and disbanded in 1763.

78th Regiment of Foot, Fraser's Highlanders: raised in 1758 and disbanded in 1763.

79th Regiment of Foot: raised in 1758 and disbanded in 1763.

80th Regiment of Foot, Light Armed: raised in 1758 and disbanded in 1764, it was a light infantry regiment.

81st Regiment of Foot, Invalids: raised in 1757 from the Invalid Corps, disbanded in 1764.

82nd Regiment of Foot, Invalids: raised in 1757 from the Invalid Corps, disbanded in 1764.

83rd Regiment of Foot: raised in 1758 and disbanded in 1763.

84th Regiment of Foot: raised in 1758 and disbanded in 1764.

85th Regiment of Foot, Volunteers Light Infantry: raised in 1759 and disbanded in 1763, it was a light infantry regiment.

86th Regiment of Foot: raised in 1759 and disbanded in 1763.

87th Regiment of Foot, Keith's Highlanders: raised in 1759 and disbanded in 1763.

88th Regiment of Foot, Campbell's Highlanders: raised in 1760 and disbanded in 1763.

89th Regiment of Foot, Morris' Highlanders: raised in 1759 and disbanded in 1763.

90th Regiment of Foot, Irish Light Infantry: raised in 1759 and disbanded in 1763, it was a light infantry regiment.

91st Regiment of Foot: raised in 1759 and disbanded in 1763.

92nd Regiment of Foot, Donegal Light Infantry: raised in 1760 and disbanded in 1763, it was a light infantry regiment.

93rd Regiment of Foot: raised in 1760 and disbanded in 1763.

94th Regiment of Foot, Royal Welsh Volunteers: raised in 1760 and disbanded in 1763.

Musketeer of the 25th Foot.

Grenadiers from various regiments, from left to right: 25th Foot, 26th Foot and 27th Foot. (*Royal Collection Trust / © His Majesty King Charles III 2024*)

95th Regiment of Foot: raised in 1760 and disbanded in 1763.

96th Regiment of Foot: raised in 1760 and disbanded in 1763.

97th Regiment of Foot: raised in 1760 and disbanded in 1763.

98th Regiment of Foot: raised in 1760 and disbanded in 1763.

99th Regiment of Foot: raised in 1760 and disbanded in 1763.

100th Regiment of Foot, Campbell's Highlanders: raised in 1761 and disbanded in 1763.

101st Regiment of Foot, Johnstone's Highlanders: raised in 1760 and disbanded in 1763.

Musketeer of the 28th Foot.

Musketeer of the 28th Foot (left) and fusilier of the 21st Foot (right).

Musketeers of the 29th Foot (left) and the 30th Foot (right).

102nd Regiment of Foot, Queen's Royal Volunteers: raised in 1760 and disbanded in 1763.

103rd Regiment of Foot, Volunteer Hunters: raised in 1761 and disbanded in 1763, it was a light infantry regiment.

104th Regiment of Foot, King's Volunteers: raised in 1761 and disbanded in 1763.

105th Regiment of Foot, Queen's Own Royal Highlanders: raised in 1761 and disbanded in 1763.

106th Regiment of Foot: raised in 1761 and disbanded in 1763.

107th Regiment of Foot, Queen's Own Royal Regiment of British Volunteers: raised in 1761 and disbanded in 1763.

108th Regiment of Foot: raised in 1760 and disbanded in 1763.

109th Regiment of Foot: raised in 1761 and disbanded in 1763.

110th Regiment of Foot, Queen's Own Musketeers: raised in 1761 and disbanded in 1763.

111th Regiment of Foot: raised in 1761 and disbanded in 1763.

112th Regiment of Foot, King's Royal Musketeers: raised in 1761 and disbanded in 1763.

113th Regiment of Foot, Royal Highlanders: raised in 1761 and disbanded in 1763.

114th Regiment of Foot, Royal Highland Volunteers: raised in 1761 and disbanded in 1763.

115th Regiment of Foot, Royal Scotch Lowlanders: raised in 1761 and disbanded in 1763.

116th Regiment of Foot, Invalids: raised in 1762 from the Invalid Corps, disbanded in 1763.

117th Regiment of Foot, Invalids: raised in 1762 from the Invalid Corps, disbanded in 1763.

118th Regiment of Foot, Invalids: raised in 1762 from the Invalid Corps, disbanded in 1763.

Musketeers of the 31st Foot (left) and the 32nd Foot (right). The 32nd Regiment of Foot was one of the few units to have a coat without frontal lapels.

Musketeers of the 33rd Foot (left) and the 34th Foot (right).

Musketeers of the 44th Foot (left) and the 45th Foot (right).

Musketeers of the 46th Foot (left) and the 47th Foot (right). The 47th Regiment of Foot was one of the few units to have a coat without frontal lapels.

Musketeers of the 48th Foot (left) and the 49th Foot (right).

Musketeer of the 50th Foot.

Fifer (left) and drummer (right) of the British line infantry. (*Royal Collection Trust / © His Majesty King Charles III 2024*)

Private of the Invalid Corps.

the crown: the Argyle Fencibles and the Sutherland Fencibles. Both units were extremely short-lived, since they were disbanded in 1763. Generally speaking, the Fencible Battalions were temporary units that were raised for active service only when Britain was fighting a major war overseas. They were made up of volunteers but were commanded by officers from the regular army.

Chapter 4

Highland Infantry

The Scottish regiments were a fundamental component of the English infantry even before the creation of Great Britain; five important units of the English Army were recruited from Scotland before 1707 (the year during which the Scottish Army was merged with the English one): the 3rd Foot Guards, the 1st Regiment of Foot, the 21st Regiment of Foot, the 25th Regiment of Foot and the 26th Regiment of Foot. All these formations, however, were recruited from the Scottish Lowlands, not from the Highlands. For this reason, they had worn, since their creation, the same uniforms as the English line infantrymen and thus were practically indistinguishable from them. The Lowlands had always been strongly linked to England and had accepted English rule in a favourable way, while the Highlands were always very jealous of their freedom and never accepted union with England. The Highlanders, who had proved themselves undoubtedly the best fighters in the British Isles, rose up against the English several times during the eighteenth century, which prevented the military authorities of Great Britain from raising regular military units from them. This situation started to change only after the crushing of the 1745 Jacobite Rebellion, which was the last great rising of the Highlanders. It was eventually possible to form several regiments of Highlanders, which soon became an elite within the British Army. Wearing their own traditional uniforms and having their own peculiar denominations, these units were completely different from the other Scottish ones raised in the Lowlands. From an organizational point of view, the Highland regiments had exactly the same structure as the standard British ones; their musicians, however, played bagpipes instead of drums. Each regiment consisted of a single battalion with nine companies of line infantrymen and one of grenadiers. Three of each regiment's companies were commanded by the field officers of the corps: a colonel (who also commanded the entire unit), lieutenant colonel (second in command for the whole regiment) and major. The major was a fundamental component of the regiment, since he was responsible for the training and discipline of all its companies. The other seven companies were commanded by captains, while a second captain could act in place of the colonel as company commander when he was absent. Each officer commanding a company was assisted by a lieutenant and an ensign, although in the grenadier company the ensign was substituted by a second lieutenant. In addition to the company officers, each regiment had four further commissioned staff officers: one adjutant, quartermaster, surgeon and chaplain. Each single company comprised three sergeants, three corporals and two bagpipers, in addition to seventy privates. The grenadier companies had two fifers as musicians, while the colonel's company had five sergeants instead of three, the two additional NCOs being a sergeant major and a quartermaster sergeant. The senior sergeant of each company also acted as pay sergeant and thus played an important administrative role. Each infantry company also had a pioneer soldier specifically trained as a combat engineer. As with the regular line infantry of the British Army, the ten pioneers of each regiment could be joined together as a single squad. Generally speaking, the Highlanders were excellent soldiers: they could be less disciplined than their English equivalents, but their courage and fitness were unrivalled. They often defended a position to the last man and were extremely proud of their regimental traditions. On many occasions they were able to achieve success despite being at a clear numerical disadvantage, and their morale was usually very high. The Highlanders were used to living in poor and rocky countryside, where living conditions were extremely harsh, so they could endure hardships of any kind while on campaign and could live for days with very little food. They were able to move very rapidly across every kind of terrain and had excellent skirmishing abilities. In combat, the Highlanders were prone to use their bayonets much more frequently than their English equivalents, their fighting spirit still being that of the ancient Celtic warriors. When needed, however, they could deliver very accurate fire upon the enemy ranks. Their talents and abilities made the Highlanders skilled light infantrymen.

The first regular military unit of Highlanders was formed in 1603, long before the formation of the British Army. It was a mounted company known as the King's Guard and was tasked with keeping the law among the warlike tribal communities of the Highlands. At the beginning of the seventeenth century, the northernmost part of Scotland was perceived as a wild country by most English officials, who experienced serious difficulties in collecting taxes from it. Cattle lifting, kidnapping and duelling were part of the Highlanders' normal activities: as a result, in 1624, it was decided to form two independent companies of infantry – recruited from Highlanders who were loyal to the government – in order to police the rural areas of northern Scotland inhabited by the Highland clans. These early units, like the previous King's Guard, were not particularly effective and were disbanded during the turbulent years of the Scottish Civil War (1644–1645). After his restoration in 1660, Charles II decided to create some new Independent Highland Companies from the Highlanders who were loyal to his rule. The first such unit was raised by the Earl of Argyll in 1666, followed in 1667 by one that was raised by the Earl of Atholl. These early companies

Private (left) and NCO (right) of the Independent Highland Companies.

Piper of the Independent Highland Companies.

had a temporary nature, usually being quite short-lived: they were formed when the Highland communities were on the verge of revolt and were disbanded when the danger had passed. In most cases they acted as the personal police of the Scottish nobles who raised and paid them. Within a few years, after becoming unhappy with the behaviour of his two Independent Highland Companies, Charles II decided to attach them to the Earl of Mar's Regiment of Foot (which was part of the Scottish Army and later became the Royal Scots Fusiliers). After his accession to the throne in 1685, James II ordered the organization of twelve independent companies in the Highlands, each of which was raised by a prominent local noble, who had to pay for all the expenses deriving from it. Some of these new companies were extremely small, having just twenty-five men instead of the planned 100. Following the Glorious Revolution, the existing independent companies were disbanded and replaced by four new ones, whose formation was ordered by William of Orange. Each of the new units, created in 1691, was to include three officers and six NCOs in addition to 100 privates. The four Highland companies were soon attached to the regular regiments of foot of the Scottish Army and were disbanded in 1694.

At the beginning of the eighteenth century, lawlessness was still a major problem in northern Scotland, many of the most important clans having remained loyal to the Stuarts after the Glorious Revolution. The English government, fearing that a local uprising could become a major national revolt of Scotland, decided to organize two new independent Scottish companies in 1701. One was raised by Clan Campbell and another by Clan Grant, both units being tasked with assisting the courts of justice and policing rural areas. A third company was added to the two existing ones in 1704. In 1707, the Highland companies became part of the newly formed British Army, until that moment having been part of the Scottish Army. During the Jacobite Rising of 1715, the independent companies played an important role in crushing the rebellion by disarming large groups of Highland insurgents. In 1717, however, they were disbanded, their members being mixed in with the British regular troops stationed in Scotland to act as guides. Following the outbreak of another Jacobite revolt in 1719, which saw the landing of a small Spanish expeditionary force on the Scottish coastline, a new Highland company was raised from Clan Munro, which performed quite well but was disbanded at the end of the hostilities. In 1724, Simon Fraser, Lord Lovat – one of Scotland's most important nobles – wrote to tell George I that the disbandment of the Highland companies in 1717 had been a great mistake since it had encouraged the outbreak of Jacobite revolts across the country's rural regions. Fraser told the monarch that the Highland clans loyal to the crown would be happy to provide their best men for the defence of law and order in Scotland. In 1725, Field Marshal George Wade assumed command of all military forces deployed

Soldiers of the 42nd Regiment of Foot (the Black Watch).

in northern Britain, and following Fraser's advice he gave instructions for the re-establishment of the Independent Highland Companies. There were six of these in total, three with 100 men each and three with 75 men. Wade soon increased the level of discipline of the new units, choosing expert officers to guide them. Individual companies was recruited from members of Clan Munro, Clan Fraser and Clan Grant, with three from members of Clan Campbell.

The six Independent Highland Companies, despite being part of the British regular forces, were permitted to wear national uniform in Highland style and to patrol the Scottish countryside according to their traditional methods. They eventually became known as the Am Freiceadan Dubh, or Black Watch, because of the dark colour of the tartan cloth with which their traditional kilts were made. In 1739, another four Independent Highland Companies were created, bringing their total number to ten. This expansion was the result of the great success of the Highland regular units, which had shown themselves to be extremely useful in patrolling the territories of the warlike clans. Also in 1739, the British government decided to merge the ten companies in order to form a Highland infantry regiment, to be known as the Earl of Crawford's Highland Regiment (which later became the 42nd Regiment of Foot). In March 1743, this new unit was assembled at Perth in preparation for moving to London, from where it was to be sent to present-day Belgium in order to fight against the French in the War of the Austrian Succession. During their march, however, some of the Highlanders mutinied, having been assured that they would never be called to serve outside Scotland. The mutineers were intercepted and punished very severely, while the rest of the regiment was sent to Flanders. Here it participated in the disastrous

Private of the 42nd Foot.

Private of the 42nd Foot.

Battle of Fontenoy, during which it fought with ferocity against the French. The outbreak of the Second Jacobite Rising in 1745 found the British authorities with no regular Highland units in Scotland, since the 42nd Regiment was serving overseas. Consequently, eighteen new Independent Highland Companies had to be raised very rapidly. These, recruited from the clans loyal to the crown, played a prominent role in crushing the new Jacobite rebellion. In particular, they countered the rebel Highlanders by employing their same methods of fighting and chased down all the Jacobite survivors after the decisive Battle of Culloden.

The good performance of the 42nd Regiment at the Battle of Fontenoy and the beginning of the Jacobite Rising convinced the British government to create a new Highland infantry regiment in 1745, known as the Earl of Loudon's Regiment of Foot. This had a large establishment of twenty companies and fought at the Battle of Culloden. In 1748, after a brief period of service overseas to fight against the French, the Earl of Loudon's Regiment of Foot was disbanded; the eighteen Independent Highland Companies, meanwhile, had already been disbanded just six months after Culloden. As a result of this, at the end of the War of the Austrian Succession, the 42nd Regiment of Foot remained the only Highland unit of the British Army. It served for a long time in Ireland until being sent to North America following the outbreak of the Seven Years' War. In the dense forests of the Thirteen Colonies, the members of the Black Watch showed all their valour, fighting with enormous courage against the French and their native allies. The Highlanders' military contribution was fundamental to the final British conquest of Canada. In 1758, the regiment formed its second battalion and received the denomination of the Royal Highland Regiment. During the Seven Years' War, nine new Highland regiments were created following the success of the Black Watch: the 77th Foot, 78th Foot, 87th Foot, 88th Foot, 89th Foot, 100th Foot, 101st Foot, 105th Foot and 114th Foot. The first two of these, raised in 1757, fought with distinction in North America, while the third and the fourth fought in Germany. The remaining regiments, like most of the new short-lived units formed during the Seven Years' War, saw little or no active service. In 1760, five Independent Highland Companies had been raised for patrolling northern Scotland, but these were soon absorbed into the 87th Regiment of Foot. In 1763, with the end of hostilities, all the new Highland units created during the Seven Years' War were disbanded, leaving the 42nd Regiment as the only remaining Highland unit in the British Army.

Chapter 5

Light Infantry

During the first four decades of the eighteenth century, line infantry formations were the most important component of European armies, making up the bulk of the troops mobilized by the various nations and acquiring a certain tactical superiority over cavalry. Highly trained and well-disciplined, they consisted of musketeers who were able to march and manoeuvre in perfect order by maintaining 'shoulder-to-shoulder' close formations. While moving on the battlefield, the line infantrymen advanced in columns; when stopping to open fire upon the enemy, they were deployed into long lines. After rolling volleys of musketry were exchanged between two opposing infantry formations, a clash could continue in two different ways: on most occasions, one of the two lines was shattered by the enemy fire and decided to retreat (usually keeping order among the ranks and readopting column formation); but on some occasions, it was necessary to fight hand-to-hand with bayonets to determine the outcome of the confrontation. Keeping order in the formations and delivering a regular fire were the key factors behind victory; as a result, training was absolutely decisive to transform line infantry into an effective tactical tool. Generally speaking, battles were extremely static, since maintaining perfect order in the formations obliged the infantrymen to move very slowly. The transition from the column formation to the line was extremely delicate, as it exposed the infantrymen to the sudden charges of cavalry. When confronting the mounted troops, line infantry usually adopted a standard defensive formation known as the square: this was another kind of close order, created many years previously with the aim of stopping enemy attacks by using the bayonets as 'pikes' against mounted troops. The formations and tactics described above were determined by the performance of the muskets that were used during the eighteenth century; these were flintlock weapons, whose loading operations were rather complicated. This meant that only one or two shots were fired in a minute, considering the standard performances of a line infantryman with good training. The flintlock muskets of this period were all smoothbores, and thus were extremely inaccurate: when a ball was fired, it came out from the weapon without a precise direction as there were no grooves inside the barrel that could guide it. A flintlock musket was of some use only when fired 100–200 metres from the target, so during a battle the line infantry formations had to come very close in order to use their weapons with some degree of effectiveness. The muskets of this age were also extremely heavy, which greatly limited the mobility of the foot soldiers. When moving across broken terrain, for example covered with rocks or trees, it was practically impossible for them to keep their close formations in order. All the main tactical formations had been created for an ideal battlefield, consisting of a large plain where the opposing infantry formations could move without encountering obstacles. In this military system, soldiers were not required to think and act in an autonomous way: they only had to move like clockwork toys in order to put into practice the orders they received. There was no space for initiative, with each infraction of discipline being immediately punished through very harsh methods. The evolutions required on the battlefield were repeated every day during training sessions, under the incessant beat of the drums. A perfect example of the kind of war that was fought in the eighteenth century was represented by the Prussian Army of Frederick the Great, which perfected close-order infantry tactics to the maximum and was admired by all the officer corps of Europe. Frederick's infantrymen were the best in Europe and their methods of training were copied by all the Continent's other armies, be they enemies or allies. During the War of the Austrian Succession in the mid-eighteenth century, however, some battles revealed that the Prussian line infantry was not as perfect as it may seem. It became apparent that it could experience serious problems while operating on broken terrain and when fighting against enemy units that employed hit-and-run guerrilla tactics. In particular, the Prussians struggled to deal with the efficient light troops deployed by the Austrian Empire, which consisted of semi-regular light infantrymen, recruited from the warlike inhabitants of the Balkans.

The light infantrymen of the Austrian Army had been fighting for decades against the Ottoman Turks on the southern frontier of the Austrian Empire, which lived in a state of endless conflict, during which both sides launched rapid incursions into the territory of their enemy to raid and pillage. The Austrian frontier soldiers had gradually learned how to fight like their enemies, becoming very expert in the art of skirmishing and scouting. Their usual area of operations was covered with mountains and woods, where each soldier had to move individually, not in column or line formation. Most of these soldiers were excellent huntsmen in their civilian life and were also farmers, living on the Balkan frontier as military settlers. Their innovative tactics derived from hunting and were based on the principle of 'open formation'. Each soldier advanced autonomously, but keeping contact with other members of his unit. By doing so, he could cover his advance behind obstacles of the terrain (like a tree, for example) and fire upon the enemy from a favourable position. On several occasions, the Austrian light infantrymen caused serious trouble and losses to

Soldiers of the 119th Foot. This was a light infantry regiment, as is clear from the crested headgear reproduced in the painting. The corps was partly equipped with pikes. (*Royal Collection Trust / © His Majesty King Charles III 2024*)

Frederick the Great's perfect line infantry. Initially, they were considered as simply murderers by the most traditionalist of their enemies, but during the course of the War of the Austrian Succession it became apparent that they could play a very important role on the battlefield. The other great powers of Europe, differently from Austria, did not have a militarized border from which expert light fighters could be recruited, so they started to create their own light infantry corps from the best hunters and gamekeepers of their communities. These new units soon assumed the denomination of Chasseurs or Jagers, terms – the first in French, the other in German – that mean 'huntsmen'. The members of these units were usually dressed in green, like most of the contemporary civilian hunters, and also like them communicated with horns and not with drums like the line infantry. During the Seven Years' War, dozens of new light formations were raised in France and Prussia, following the Austrian example, and showed great efficiency on campaign, confirming that a new branch of the infantry had effectively been born.

The conflict of 1756–1763 was also fought in the Americas, with the clash between the British and the French colonies in the northern part of the New World. In North America, the tactical situation encountered by the European armies was completely different from that of Europe, some form of local light infantry having already existed there for more or less a century. The terrain of Britain's Thirteen Colonies, as well as that of French Canada (New France), was mostly covered with dense forests and was inhabited by native communities whose warriors all fought as lightly armed and highly mobile skirmishers. Colonial warfare consisted of swift raids and incursions launched across the frontier, exactly like on the southern border of the Austrian Empire. As a result, each British or French colonist/farmer was also a militiaman with great skirmishing capabilities. In order to survive, each settler had to learn hunting in the forests and fighting against the natives by using their same methods. In the late seventeenth century, the first great war in the history of Colonial America was fought between

Private of a light infantry company during the Seven Years' War.

the English colonists and the native tribes. The 1675 conflict is commonly known as King Philip's War, from the nickname that the colonists gave to their main native opponent (a great leader whose true name was Metacomet). The war consisted of a major native insurgency that took place on the borders of the English colonies, which could have potentially led to the expulsion of the colonists from that part of North America. Using their hit-and-run guerrilla tactics, the native warriors of Metacomet caused many losses to the colonial militia and destroyed a large number of English settlements. Learning from bitter experience, the colonial authorities realized that they would have to create a light infantry corps that could oppose the native attacks by using their same tactics. Command of this experimental new unit was given to Benjamin Church, a settler with extensive combat experience, and its members were formed into a single company and were known as rangers. During the second half of the conflict, Benjamin Church's men obtained a series of victories over the natives and eventually killed Metacomet during a forest skirmish, making the rangers a key factor behind the final victory of the colonists.

From 1675, all the colonies of North America started to have their own chosen units of rangers, which were deployed on the frontier with the native territories: light infantry was thus born in the New World. What had been achieved in North America, however, was not learned in Europe. No English troops had participated in King Philip's War, so Benjamin Church's innovations did not reach Europe. At that time, the American Thirteen Colonies were considered as a secondary theatre of operations, and this did not change until the outbreak of the Seven Years' War. It should be noted, however, that most of the new ranger corps raised in the colonies after 1675 were 'rangers' in the true sense of the word rather than elite skirmishers like those commanded by Church: their main task was to patrol the countryside of their colonies, especially the areas bordering native lands. These frontier rangers were frequently mounted and thus acted more as a police force than as proper soldiers. Church's rangers of 1675–1676 consisted of 200 volunteers assembled into an independent company; sixty of these were colonists while the remaining 140 were friendly natives. These native allies trained their white companions and transmitted to them all the skills needed for bush fighting. Church was an experienced scout and woodland fighter who understood that the only way to obtain decisive victories against the hostile natives was to fight by using the same combat tactics as his enemies. His company of rangers was created to penetrate deep into enemy territory in order to conduct retaliatory raids or to gather precious intelligence about the movements of the natives. Church's men were all equipped as light infantrymen, like their native opponents. They wore comfortable moccasins to enable them to walk or run rapidly in the woods and were armed with hatchets for hand-to-hand fighting against native

Private of the Nova Scotia Rangers, wearing the second uniform of its corps. (*Colour plate by Herbert Knotel. Part of the Anne S.K. Brown Military Collection*)

warriors armed with tomahawks. They moved on horseback when possible and were also trained to travel by canoe. All rangers were excellent marksmen and could reload their muskets very rapidly. During the War of the Grand Alliance and the War of the Spanish Succession, the independent company of rangers guided by Benjamin Church was re-formed, but it always remained a temporary corps and was finally disbanded after Church's retirement from military service. Between 1710 and 1713, another short-lived unit of rangers, comprising friendly Mohawk natives commanded by two white officers, was created to garrison Port-Royal in Nova Scotia. It was not until 1744, however, that another unit of rangers comparable to Church's original one was formed.

In that year, three small companies of Nova Scotia Rangers, each with sixty men, were raised in Massachusetts and sent to Nova Scotia to reinforce the local garrison. Nova Scotia was particularly exposed to frequent attacks by local natives who were loyal allies of the French. The Canadian outpost had previously been part of the French dominions in North America, under the name of Acadia, and the French nurtured ambitions of reconquering it. On the border of Nova Scotia were some Jesuit missions, which the French used as their bases to coordinate the raids of their native allies against the British settlements. The Nova Scotia Rangers were specifically created to face the menace represented by the French and their native allies, and soon became known as Goreham's Rangers from the name of their skilled commander, Captain John Goreham. Most members of its three companies were Mohawks or individuals of mixed-blood who knew how to fight in the difficult environment of Nova Scotia. The original three companies were reduced to one, which had a larger establishment with 130 rangers and eight officers. Goreham's Rangers served with distinction during the French-Indian War (the North American theatre of the Seven Years' War), to the point of being made part of the British Army's regular establishment with the new denomination of the North American Rangers. Goreham's men were the first rangers to receive this honour in the military history of Colonial America. The corps was later expanded to two companies, one garrisoned in Nova Scotia and the other in New Brunswick, before being disbanded in 1763. In 1755, after the outbreak of the French-Indian War, the most famous unit of colonial rangers was formed in New Hampshire: Roger's Rangers. These originated from a single company that was detached from one of the ordinary militia regiments in order to perform scouting duties, which was commanded by Captain Robert Rogers. By the spring of 1756, the new unit had already shown its great potential, and consisted of one captain, one lieutenant, one ensign, three sergeants and sixty rangers. Roger's Rangers were formally a Provincial unit that was re-enlisted every year; differently from the other Provincials, however, they were paid by the British government. During 1756, the unit was greatly expanded, with the formation of another four companies (one of which was entirely made up of friendly Stockbridge natives). At the beginning of 1757 the internal composition of the individual companies was increased as follows: one captain, one lieutenant, one ensign, four sergeants and 100 rangers. During 1757, the number of companies was increased to nine; the rangers were so effective in their scouting operations that their commander, Robert Rogers, was ordered to train one company of British regulars (all volunteers) like he did with his own rangers. In 1758, another six companies of rangers, paid by the British, were raised in New England, two of these being made up of friendly Stockbridge natives. In November 1760, with the fall of French Canada, almost all the companies of rangers returned to New England and were disbanded, two continuing to serve until 1761. Thanks to the military events of 1755–1760, the British government understood that some corps of rangers were absolutely vital in North America in order to counter the threat of the native tribes. As a result, in 1762, Captain Joseph Hopkins was ordered to raise a new corps of rangers from Maryland and Pennsylvania. This new unit was known as the Queen's Royal American Rangers and was placed on the regular establishment of the British Army. It consisted of two officers and 100 men, thus having the numerical consistency of a company. The Queen's Royal American Rangers played a prominent role during Pontiac's Rebellion, which commenced shortly after Canada was included in the British colonial possessions. The rebellion involved most of the native tribes that had fought with the French during the French-Indian War, who had no intention of accepting British rule. The new corps of rangers was disbanded at the end of 1763.

The light infantry revolution caused by the French-Indian War did not see only the formation of the colonial ranger units described above, as it also affected very deeply the structure of the British line infantry. In 1755, the British government decided to create the first regular light infantry unit of the British Army, a step mostly taken because of the disastrous defeat suffered by the British line infantry in 1754 at the Battle of Monogahela. This saw the ambush of 1,300 British soldiers by a smaller force of French and natives. The British contingent included line infantrymen from the 44th and 48th Foot, in addition to Provincial soldiers of the Virginia Regiment commanded by a young George Washington. The clash was a disaster for the British, who lost over 450 men during the ambush and proved unable to react effectively to the enemy skirmishing tactics. The new light infantry unit created after the Battle of Monogahela was initially known as the 62nd Regiment of Foot (the Royal Americans), only adopting its definitive progressive number (the 60th) in 1757. Approval for the raising of the new regiment, as well as the funds needed for it, were granted by the British Parliament in late 1755. The unit comprised four battalions of

Private of Rogers' Rangers, wearing the fringed hunting shirt used on campaign. (*Colour plate by Herbert Knotel, part of the Anne S.K. Brown Military Collection*)

1,000 soldiers each, and its main function was to counter the raids launched by the French and by their native allies against the settlements of the Thirteen Colonies. The regiment was recruited from colonists who already had experience of light infantry tactics as well as foreigners who had hunting capabilities. In particular, the British Army was interested in recruiting German hunters and gamekeepers, like those who were already serving in the light units of the Prussian and French armies. To allow the recruitment of such experienced personnel, the British Parliament passed the Commissions to Foreign Protestants Act in 1756 that permitted the enlisting of foreign officers from the German states and Swiss cantons. These were employed in the new 62nd Foot, but could not rise above the rank of lieutenant colonel. In total, some fifty officers of the regiment came from Germany or Switzerland, although overall command of the unit was given to General John Campbell (at that time commander-in-chief of the British Army in North America).

The original idea behind the formation of the new unit had been that of Jacques Prevost, a Swiss soldier and adventurer who was a personal friend of the Duke of Cumberland (second son of King George II). Prevost was an expert in forest warfare and was one of the first to understand the combat potential of light infantry. In essence, the Royal American Regiment united the main features of a Provincial (colonial) corps with those of a foreign (mercenary) one. It merged the light infantry traditions of North America (the rangers) with those of Central Europe (jagers). All members of the unit were Protestants, which was a deliberate move since their main opponents were French Catholics. Curiously, the Royal American Regiment was the first British unit to have foreign officers, but did not comprise any officer from the American colonies. The foreign officers of the regiment included two notable personalities: Henri Bouquet (who commanded the 1st Battalion) and Frederick Haldimand (who commanded the 2nd Battalion). Both these Swiss professionals made a great contribution to the development of light infantry doctrines within the British Army, their forward-looking ideas including the introduction (unofficially for the moment) of rifled muskets among the rankers. These new weapons, which had long barrels with spiral grooves in the bore, had started to be produced on a small scale during the early eighteenth century. They had become popular in the American colonies thanks to the German gunsmiths who migrated to the New World and brought these new muskets with them. Thanks to their superior precision, the rifles were the ideal weapon for hunting and fighting in the woods of North America, and in consequence they were gradually adopted as personal weapons of choice by all the colonists/militiamen of the Thirteen Colonies. For a long time, however, this superior type of flintlock musket was not adopted by European armies, continuing to be used only for hunting around Europe. During the Seven Years' War, however, some of the

Private of Rogers' Rangers, wearing winter campaign dress. Snowshoes were used quite frequently during winter. (*Colour plate by Herbert Knotel, part of the Anne S.K. Brown Military Collection*)

newly formed light corps of the European armies started to adopt rifled carbines, more or less at the same time as many soldiers from the Royal American Regiment began substituting their smoothbores with rifled muskets. The production costs of the new muskets were quite high, but using such a weapon could determine the outcome of a battle due to its high level of accuracy. The French-Indian War was the first conflict during which rifles were used on a large scale, but it would take another eighty years to see the adoption of rifled muskets by the line infantry. Bouquet and Haldimand also modified the standard uniforms of the British line infantry in order to make them more comfortable for light infantry use. The long tails of the coat were shortened to increase mobility, and the coloured lapels on the front of the uniform were buttoned up to be more practical. During the French-Indian War, the 60th Foot fought with enormous courage during several important engagements, earning a solid reputation and the famous motto *'Celer et Audax'* ('swift and bold'). In 1762, Parliament, in order to keep its soldiers in the ranks of the British military, passed the American Protestant Soldier Naturalization Act, which offered naturalization to all those foreign officers and soldiers who had already served under the Union Jack for at least two years. Armed with rifled muskets and hatchets, the forest fighters of the Royal American Regiment also fought to put down Pontiac's Rebellion.

Following the success of the 60th Foot, in 1758 each British line infantry battalion was ordered to train one of its line companies as light infantry. By 1763, most of the British infantry battalions had their own light company, which was usually formed by assembling together the youngest and fittest members of each unit. The light infantrymen, thanks to their superior mobility and excellent marksmanship, soon assumed an elite status comparable to that of the grenadiers. Light companies from different regiments were frequently brought together to form temporary Light Battalions that were used to perform special missions. On the field of battle, the light company of each infantry battalion was deployed on the left while the grenadier company was on the right, as a result of which the grenadier and light infantry companies became known as flank companies. The light company of each battalion usually acted as the advance guard during a march and as the rearguard when retreating. During the Seven Years' War, the British formed another six light infantry regiments in addition to the 60th Foot: the 80th Foot, 85th Foot, 90th Foot, 92nd Foot, 103rd Foot and 119th Foot. The 80th Foot was raised by Colonel Thomas Gage in May 1758, following the success of the 60th Foot and of the Cadet Company of British regulars (all volunteers) who were retrained as light infantrymen by Robert Rogers. The 80th Foot was a ranger regiment designed for operating in the woods of North America, which was reflected in its peculiar uniform, and which included a jockey's cap made of black leather and a short brown coat. Colonel Gage's unit fought with distinction in the French-Indian War and later took part in Pontiac's Rebellion. The 85th Foot, commanded by Colonel John Craufurd, was the first light infantry unit of the British Army to be recruited in Great Britain (the 60th Foot and 80th Foot had been raised in North America). Along with the 90th Foot, it saw some action in northern France before the end of the Seven Years' War. The 92nd Foot and 119th Foot never fought, while the 103rd Foot only participated in a minor action in northern France. With the end of the Seven Years' War, all the light infantry regiments were disbanded, except for the 60th Foot; even the 80th Foot, which had served with distinction, was not retained in service. The light infantry companies of the various line regiments reverted to their pre-1758 status in 1763, as if nothing had been learned from the combat experiences of the Seven Years' War. In 1771, however, one light infantry company was re-formed in each line infantry battalion.

Chapter 6

Guard Cavalry

Like all the major European military forces in the early eighteenth century, the British Army included some cavalry units that had 'guard' status. These acted as the mounted bodyguard of the royal family and were considered to be the elite of the British heavy cavalry. In 1727, there were seven British guard cavalry units: four troops of Life Guards, two companies of Horse Grenadiers and one regiment of Horse Guards. The history of the Life Guards began in 1658, when England and Scotland were still two independent realms ruled by the same monarch; as a result, they were originally part of the English Army. The 1st Troop of Life Guards was raised in 1658 as part of the forces organized by Charles II during his exile in the Spanish Netherlands, the elite cavalry formation comprising some of the Stuart monarch's most loyal followers. During the same year, the 2nd Troop of Life Guards was established, with the official denomination of The Duke of York's Troop of Horse Guards. The 3rd Troop of Life Guards was added in 1659, this being commonly known as Monck's Lifeguards as it acted as the mounted bodyguard of George Monck, the main political supporter of Charles II during his exile. The members of the three Lifeguard units were known as 'gentlemen', since they all came from the higher social classes of England and were required to provide their own horses and uniforms. In 1660, with the restoration of the monarchy, Charles II returned to England to take the throne, after which the Life Guards were absorbed into the reorganized English Army and continued to act as the mounted bodyguard of the king. In 1678, one company of horse grenadiers was added to each troop of Life Guards, these being made up of ordinary soldiers rather than 'gentlemen'. During the late seventeenth century, horse grenadiers became increasingly popular in European armies, together with their foot equivalents. Around 1670, the first corps of horse grenadiers started to appear in some armies. These were not truly cavalry units, since their members acted as mounted infantrymen: they used their horses to travel long distances but usually dismounted to fight. Indeed, it was practically impossible to throw hand-grenades accurately from horseback. With the addition of the three companies of horse grenadiers, the numerical establishment of the Life Guards became significantly larger. The 'gentlemen' did not have a high opinion of their new 'plebeian' comrades, but the latter provided important tactical support to

Trooper of the 1st Life Guards. (*Royal Collection Trust / © His Majesty King Charles III 2024*)

the traditional cavalry thanks to their peculiar weaponry. The internal composition of a troop of Life Guards was as follows: one captain, four lieutenants, one cornet, one guidon, one quartermaster, four brigadiers, four sub-brigadiers, four trumpeters, one kettledrummer and 200 'gentlemen'. The companies of horse grenadiers had two

Troopers of the 1st Life Guards (left) and the 2nd Life Guards (right).

lieutenants, two sergeants, two corporals, two drummers, four hautboys and sixty-four privates. In 1686, the 4th Troop of Life Guards, with an attached company of horse grenadiers, was raised by James II.

In addition to the four units described above, which were all part of the English Army, there was also a Scottish corps of Life Guards, which was formed by Viscount Newburgh shortly after the Restoration of Charles II in 1661. Originally, the unit had an establishment of four officers, five NCOs, one surgeon, one clerk, three trumpeters, one kettledrummer and 120 troopers. The 2nd Troop of Scottish Life Guards was raised soon after the first, but this had a very short history as it was disbanded in 1676. During James II's reign, Ireland also had an independent Troop of Life Guards, which had an attached company of grenadiers like the English units. This was quartered in Dublin and acted as the mounted bodyguard of the king when he was in Ireland. After the Glorious Revolution, the internal organization of the Life Guards was changed in a significant way. The armies of England, Scotland and Ireland remained independent from each other, but the new English king,

Troopers of the 3rd Life Guards (left) and the 4th Life Guards (right).

William of Orange, rationalized their internal structure. The English 4th Troop of Life Guards, which had recently been formed by James II, was disbanded in 1689. During the following ten years, it was replaced by a foreign military unit from the Netherlands that was on English pay: the Garde du Corps. William of Orange was also the ruler of the Netherlands, and the invasion force with which he landed in England was mostly made up of Dutch units. Being unsure of the loyalty of his new subjects, William retained several Dutch units on English pay long after the end of the Glorious Revolution. The Garde du Corps, also known as the 4th Troop of Life Guards, returned to its homeland only in 1699. The Scottish Life Guards remained loyal to James II during the Glorious Revolution, most of them resigning their military positions, but William of Orange soon after reorganized the unit with new 'gentlemen' who were loyal to his cause. The troop of Irish Life Guards was permanently disbanded because its members followed James II into exile and continued to serve the deposed monarch in France as part of his army in exile.

In 1707, the English Army was merged with the Scottish Army in order to form the new British Army, in consequence of which the Scottish Life Guards were amalgamated with their English equivalent and became the new 4th Troop of Life Guards. Meanwhile, in 1693, the three troops of English horse grenadiers had been assembled into a single unit known as the Horse Grenadier Guards, which had the numerical establishment of a single troop but was completely independent from the 'gentlemen' of the Life Guards. In 1702, a troop of horse grenadiers was raised in Scotland and attached to the Scottish Life Guards, but when the latter became part of the British Army in 1707, it was detached from its 'mother corps' and became an independent unit. As a result, the new British Army had a 1st and 2nd Troop of Horse Grenadiers in addition to the four troops of Life Guards. From their foundation, the Life Guards had a distinct heavy cavalry nature, and this was also gradually acquired by the troops of horse grenadiers, which abandoned the use of hand-grenades and became ordinary heavy cavalry units. In 1746, the 3rd and 4th Troops of Life Guards were disbanded following the outbreak of the Jacobite Rebellion. In 1788, as part of the great organizational changes that took place after the British military defeat in the American Revolution, it was decided to assemble the two remaining troops of Life Guards with the two troops of Horse Grenadiers in order to form two consolidated regiments: the 1st and 2nd Regiments of Life Guards. The 1st Regiment was formed by merging the 1st Troop of Life Guards and 1st Troop of Horse Grenadiers, while the 2nd Regiment was created from the 2nd Troop of Life Guards and the 2nd Troop of Horse Grenadiers. With this important organizational change, the nature of the Life Guards changed; the two new regiments started to comprise ordinary soldiers and thus were no longer made up of young 'gentlemen', as had been the case in the past. Most of the aristocrats who were still serving in the Life Guards were pensioned off, and the two new units thereafter started to comprise common soldiers who had distinguished themselves for their valour and discipline.

The Horse Guards, commonly known as The Blues because of their distinctive dark blue uniforms, had a completely different history from the two regiments of Life Guards. In 1650, while Oliver Cromwell was at the peak of his power, a heavy cavalry unit known as the Regiment of Cuirassiers was raised by Sir Arthur Haselrig. From the outset, this corps had a distinct elite status and was mostly employed to perform escort and policing duties, meaning it had more or less the same main functions as the later French Gendarmerie. With the Restoration of Charles II in 1660, the Regiment of Cuirassiers was transferred to royal service but most of its officers (who were still loyal to the Parliamentarian cause) were replaced by new ones who were loyal to the Stuarts. The unit initially consisted of just three troops, whose members were mostly wealthy gentlemen, but by the outbreak of the Glorious

Troopers of the 1st Horse Grenadier Guards (left) and the 2nd Horse Grenadier Guards (right).

Revolution it had eight troops and had received the new official denomination of The King's Regiment of Horse. Shortly before the Glorious Revolution, the regiment received 'guard' status, but when William of Orange landed in England its members abandoned James II and sided with the Dutch pretender to the English throne. During the early decades of the eighteenth century, the regiment continued to serve mostly as a policing corps, garrisoning various areas of southern Britain and preventing the outbreak of local rebellions. In 1743, following Britain's involvement in the War of the Austrian Succession, the regiment fought with distinction at the Battle of Dettingen. The British forces that were sent across the English Channel

Trooper of the Royal Horse Guards.

to fight against France comprised, for the first time, a Household Brigade, which was made up of elements from the Life Guards and the Horse Grenadiers as well as the Horse Guards (the latter, at that time, were still simply known by the name of their commanding colonel). At Dettingen, the Household Brigade showed great discipline and courage. In 1745, The Blues also participated in the Battle of Fontenoy, during which they suffered heavy casualties but could not avoid the defeat of the British forces. The Blues received their new official name of the Regiment of Royal Horse Guards in 1750, under which they fought in the Seven Years' War. During

Trooper of the Royal Horse Guards. (*Royal Collection Trust / © His Majesty King Charles III 2024*)

this conflict, the unit distinguished itself in three important battles: Minden (1759), Warburg (1760) and Villinghausen (1761). When the regiment returned to Britain in 1763 at the end of hostilities, it had lost most of its most experienced troops due to heavy casualties, as a result of which the Royal Horse Guards had to be completely reorganized. In 1788, after spending several years patrolling the countryside of the East Midlands, the Royal Horse Guards were transferred to London as part of the reorganization of the Life Guards. The government, not completely sure about the reliability of the newly reorganized Life Guards regiments, thus decided to deploy The Blues in the capital in order to count on their experience. Until that moment,

Trooper of the Royal Horse Guards.

as we have seen, the Royal Horse Guards had mostly been employed to perform internal policing duties, but had also seen substantial fighting overseas.

The troops of Life Guards had the following internal establishment: one colonel, one first lieutenant colonel, one second lieutenant colonel, one first major, one second major, four additional officers known as 'exempts', four brigadiers, four sub-brigadiers, one adjutant, two drummers and eighty troopers. The troops of Horse Grenadiers, meanwhile, comprised the following: two lieutenants, three sergeants, three corporals, two drummers and sixty troopers. The Life Guards thus had a surplus of officers within their troops. The Horse Guards were organized as a standard heavy cavalry regiment of the British Army, on six troops (sometimes supplemented by an additional seventh depot troop in the ordinary regiments, which was responsible for recruitment). Each troop comprised the following elements: one captain, one lieutenant, one cornet, three sergeants, three corporals, two drummers, one hautboy and fifty-nine troopers. The three senior troops were commanded by the field officers of each regiment, with one colonel, one lieutenant colonel and one major. On most occasions, however, the senior troop of a regiment was commanded by a captain lieutenant rather than the colonel.

Chapter 7

Heavy Cavalry

In 1727, at the time of George II's assumption of the crown, the British heavy cavalry consisted of two distinct categories: horse regiments and dragoon regiments. From a formal point of view, horse regiments were made up of heavy horsemen and dragoon regiments comprised medium horsemen, but in practice there was very little difference between the two categories since both were trained and equipped to act as shock cavalry. A real tactical difference existed only between them and the regiments of Light Dragoons (which will be covered in the next chapter). Since the days of the Restoration (1660), the English cavalry had been made up of horse regiments and dragoon regiments. Horse regiments were equipped with cuirasses until the late seventeenth century and consisted of true heavy cavalry, whereas dragoon regiments were originally raised as mounted infantry formations that were not tasked with conducting frontal charges. Initially, dragoons were introduced in post-1648 European armies as chosen units of infantrymen who could use horses to travel long distance or to move around the battlefield, but who dismounted to fight. In practice, they consisted of infantrymen with a higher degree of mobility, as indicated by their personal equipment – they were armed with long infantry muskets and did not have the same leather boots used by the cavalrymen of the horse regiments. Over time, most notably during the first decades of the eighteenth century, the dragoons gradually lost their original mounted infantry nature and were transformed into regular line cavalry. At the same time, the horse regiments discarded their metal cuirasses and started to use lighter personal equipment. As a result of these changes, the existing tactical differences that distinguished horse regiments from dragoon regiments practically ceased to exist. Neither heavy horsemen nor dragoons wore cuirasses, and they were now employed to perform the same duties. In 1727, the British Army comprised seven regiments of horse and fourteen regiments of dragoons; the members of the latter were paid less than the heavy cavalrymen, but except for this all the twenty-one units had the same basic features. Each horse or dragoon regiment was structured on six troops (sometimes supplemented by an additional seventh depot troop to aid in recruitment). Each troop was composed of the following elements: one captain, one lieutenant, one cornet, three sergeants, three corporals, two drummers, one hautboy and fifty-nine troopers. The three senior

Troopers of the 1st Horse (left) and the 2nd Horse (right).

troops were commanded by the field officers of each regiment: a colonel, lieutenant colonel and major. However, the senior troop of a regiment was usually commanded by a captain lieutenant, not by the colonel. Each mounted regiment also had a farrier, who was tasked with finishing off wounded horses and was equipped with an axe for this duty.

In 1746, the British government decided to transform the horse regiments into dragoon formations in order to cut costs and eliminate a differentiation that no longer existed in practice. The heavier mounts of the horse regiments had a considerable cost but produced no real advantages on the field of battle, while the soldiers of the horse regiments had the privilege of being paid much more than those of the dragoon units for no real reason but tradition. In order to preserve – at least formally – the elite status of the horse regiments, upon being converted into dragoon units they were given the new honorific denomination of Dragoon Guards. This meant very little in practice, since it was done only to show that the former horse regiments were older than the dragoon units. The first two horse regiments that received the new denomination of Dragoon Guards were the King's Own Regiment of Horse and the Queen's Own Regiment of Horse, which respectively became the 1st Dragoon Guards and the 2nd Dragoon Guards. In 1747, a third unit, the Prince of Wales' Own Regiment of Horse, was converted into the 3rd Dragoon Guards. The remaining four regiments of horse, which were placed on the Irish Establishment, rejected the idea of being converted into Dragoon Guard units; as a result, they were renumbered as the 1st–4th Regiments of Horse. In 1788, however, when the British

Trooper of the 3rd Horse.

cavalry was totally reorganized, the regiments of horse on the Irish Establishment were also converted into Dragoon Guard units (numbered the 4th–7th). With the creation of the Dragoon Guards, the British government found a good compromise: the costly horse regiments were abolished, but at the same time their members kept alive the glorious traditions of the British heavy cavalry.

Troopers of the 3rd Horse (left) and the 4th Horse (right).

What follows are brief unit histories for each of the regiments of British heavy cavalry existing between 1727 and 1760.

The King's Own Regiment of Horse: raised in 1685, it was originally named the Queen's Own Regiment of Horse in honour of Queen Mary (the consort of James II). With the outbreak of the Glorious Revolution, it joined William of Orange's cause, taking part in the Battle of the Boyne (1690) and the Battle of Aughrim (1691). Shortly before the birth of the British Army, it participated in all the most important battles fought by Marlborough during the War of the Spanish Succession: Blenheim (1704), Ramilies (1706), Oudenarde (1708) and Malplaquet (1709). In 1714, with the arrival of the House of Hanover in Great Britain, it was renamed as the King's Own Regiment of Horse in honour of the new King George I. With this new denomination, the unit fought at the Battle of Dettingen in 1743 during the War of the Austrian Succession. During this conflict, and following the outbreak of the Jacobite Rebellion in Scotland, it was transformed into the 1st Regiment of Dragoon Guards. In 1760, during the Seven Years' War, the corps distinguished itself at the Battle of Corbach and the Battle of Warburg.

The Queen's Own Regiment of Horse: raised in 1685, it was originally called the Earl of Peterborough's Regiment of Horse. During the Glorious Revolution,

Trooper of the 5th Horse.

it joined William of Orange's cause, fighting at the Battle of the Boyne (1690) and the Battle of Aughrim (1691). During the War of the Spanish Succession, it was sent to Portugal in order to fight against the Bourbon forces operating in the Iberian Peninsula, taking part in the Battle of Almenar (1710). After returning

Troopers of the 5th Horse (left) and the 6th Horse (right).

home, the regiment contributed to the suppression of the 1715 Jacobite Rising; in 1746, following the Second Jacobite Rebellion that was crushed at the Battle of Culloden, it became the 2nd Regiment of Dragoon Guards. In 1760, during the Seven Years' War, the unit fought well at the Battle of Corbach and Battle of Warburg. Later, during the same conflict, it fought brilliantly at the Battle of Wilhelmsthal (1762).

The Prince of Wales' Own Regiment of Horse: raised in 1685, it was originally named the Earl of Plymouth's Regiment of Horse. After the end of the Glorious Revolution, it served with distinction during the War of the Spanish Succession, taking part in the following battles: Schellenberg (1704), Blenheim (1704), Ramilies (1706), Oudenarde (1708) and Malplaquet (1709). In 1747, it was transformed into the 3rd Regiment of Dragoon Guards.

1st Regiment of Irish Horse: raised in 1685, it was originally known as the Earl of Arran's Regiment of Horse. With the outbreak of the Glorious Revolution, it joined William of Orange's cause, taking part in the Battle of the Boyne (1690) and some subsequent actions in Ireland. In 1746, the unit was transferred to the Irish Establishment of the British Army, of which it remained part until being

Trooper of the 7th Horse.

transferred back to the English Army in 1788. In that same year, it became the 4th Regiment of Dragoon Guards.

2nd Regiment of Irish Horse: raised in 1686, it was initially named the Earl of Shrewsbury's Regiment of Horse. It joined William of Orange's cause during the Glorious Revolution and took part in the Battle of the Boyne (1690) and the First Siege of Limerick (1690). During the long War of the Spanish Succession, the regiment fought at the Battle of Blenheim (1704) as well as those at Ramilies (1706) and Malplaquet (1708). During the following eighty years, it remained on garrison duty in Ireland without seeing action overseas. In 1788, the corps became the new 5th Regiment of Dragoon Guards.

3rd Regiment of Irish Horse: raised in 1686, it was originally called Lord Lumley's Regiment of Horse. With the outbreak of the Glorious Revolution, it joined William of Orange's cause and went to Ireland to fight against the Jacobite forces. Later, it was sent to continental Europe and participated in the War of the Grand Alliance, which was fought between France and a large multinational coalition of states that included England. In 1692, the unit was renamed as the King's Regiment of Carabineers, and it was with this denomination that it took part in the War of the Spanish Succession. During the latter conflict, it fought at Blenheim (1704) and Ramilies (1706). In 1745, it was part of the British forces that crushed the Jacobite Rising. Some years later, it was transferred to the Irish Establishment of the British Army, remained part of it until 1788, when it was transferred back to the English Army and transformed into the 6th Regiment of Dragoon Guards.

4th Regiment of Irish Horse: raised in 1688, it was first known as Lord Cavendish's Regiment of Horse. Despite being organized to provide a mounted escort for Princess Anne, the younger daughter of James II, the unit soon joined William of Orange when he landed in England. During the Williamite Wars that were fought in Ireland between the new English monarch and the Jacobite rebels, the regiment took part in the Battle of the Boyne (1690) before being sent to continental Europe, where it participated in the Grand Alliance War and operated against the French forces of Louis XIV. The corps returned to continental Europe with the outbreak of the War of the Spanish Succession, during which it fought with distinction at Blenheim (1704), Elixheim (1705), Ramilies (1706) and Malplaquet (1709). After the end of hostilities, the unit spent several years in Ireland, where it acted as a garrison corps. In 1742, the horsemen of the regiment were sent to the Continent again after the outbreak of the War of the Austrian Succession, participating in the Battle of Dettingen in 1743 and the Battle of Fontenoy in 1745. After a period of garrison duty in Ireland, the unit was sent to mainland Europe to fight in the Seven Years' War, fighting with distinction at the Battle of Warburg in 1760. In 1788, it was transformed into the 7th Regiment of Dragoon Guards.

1st Dragoons: this regiment, the oldest dragoon unit of the British Army, was organized in 1661 (shortly after the Restoration of Charles II) from veterans of the disbanded Parliamentary Army. It initially consisted of just one troop, but was later expanded to four before being sent to serve in Tangier. Located on the coastline of Morocco, Tangier was an English colony during the years 1661–1684 and needed a garrison in order to be defended from attacks by England's colonial rivals. The four troops of dragoons, collectively known as the Tangier Horse, served in Morocco until 1678, and were later sent to Scotland to police the Covenanters (members of a Presbyterian movement that caused political troubles to the central government). In 1680, the unit was disbanded and its men were sent back to Tangier as reinforcements for the garrison, but in 1683 they returned to England and were reorganized as an independent regiment of dragoons. This was expanded to six troops and assumed the new denomination of The Royal Regiment of Dragoons. Like most of the English military, after the outbreak of the Glorious Revolution it became part of the army of William of Orange and as such it participated in the Battle of the Boyne and the First Siege of Limerick (both in 1690). During the War of the Austrian Succession, it fought at the Battle of Dettingen (1743) and Battle of Fontenoy (1745). In 1751, it assumed the definitive denomination of the 1st Royal Regiment of Dragoons. The regiment also took part in the Seven Years' War and fought with distinction at the Battle of Warburg in 1760.

2nd Dragoons: this regiment was originally raised in 1678 as three independent troops of dragoons that were part of the Scottish Army. At that time, Scotland still had an independent army, which was mostly used to perform internal police duties. In 1681, another three troops of dragoons were raised and were assembled together with the existing ones to form a new unit that assumed the denomination of the Royal Regiment of Scots Dragoons. During this early phase of its history, the unit was already mounted on grey horses, later receiving its famous nickname of the Scots Greys. With the outbreak of the Glorious Revolution, like the rest of the Scottish Army, the Royal Regiment of Scots

Trooper of the 1st Dragoons.

Dragoons sided with William of Orange and helped him in crushing the revolt of the Scottish Jacobites. During the War of the Spanish Succession, as part of the Scottish Army, the regiment fought under Marlborough's orders with great distinction. At that time, the dragoons were still mostly employed as mounted infantrymen, and as such participated in the following battles: Schellenberg

Trooper of the 2nd Dragoons (the Scots Greys), the only unit of the British line cavalry wearing mitre caps.

Trooper of the 2nd Dragoons.

Troopers of the 3rd Dragoons (left) and the 4th Dragoons (right).

(1704), Blenheim (1704), Elixheim (1705), Ramilies (1706), Oudenarde (1708) and Malplaquet (1709). After assuming the new denomination of the Royal North British Dragoons, the regiment was absorbed with the rest of the Scottish Army into the new British Army. After returning to their homeland, the Scots Greys remained loyal to the House of Hanover during the Jacobite Rising of 1715. The Scottish dragoons fought with great determination against the rebels and were one of the key factors behind the final victory of the British forces. After the end of the rebellion in 1719, the regiment remained for more than two decades on garrison duty in Scotland and continued to perform the main duty for which it had been created: policing Scotland and preventing the outbreak of risings among the Highland clans. In 1742, two years after the beginning of the War of the Austrian Succession, the Scots Greys were sent to the Continent to fight against the French. Like several other British cavalry units, the regiment fought at Dettingen in 1743 and Fontenoy in 1745; during the latter battle, the Scots Greys covered the retreat of the defeated British infantry. When the Jacobite Rising of 1745 began, the corps was not transferred to Scotland, continuing to serve overseas until the end of the War of the Austrian Succession in 1748. During 1755, for a very short period, a single company of light cavalry was added to the establishment of the regiment, but this was soon detached

Troopers of the 5th Dragoons (left) and the 6th Dragoons (right).

from it and became an independent corps. With the outbreak of the Seven Years' War, the Scots Greys were sent to Germany, where they operated with the forces of Hanover. In 1759, the regiment participated in the clashes of Bergen and Minden, during which it had little opportunity to show its valour. During the following year, however, the Scots Greys conducted a brilliant frontal charge at the Battle of Warburg which was decisive for the outcome of the clash. Before the end of the conflict, in 1762, the Scottish regiment took part in the Battle of Wilhelmsthal, during which it attacked the French troops which had already been routed (capturing many prisoners and even part of the French baggage train).

3rd Dragoons: raised in 1685 as the Queen's Regiment of Dragoons, it originally consisted of six troops and soon joined William of Orange when he landed in England at the outbreak of the Glorious Revolution. During 1690 and 1691, the unit fought against the Jacobites in Ireland, before being sent to continental Europe to participate in the Grand Alliance War. With the beginning of the new century, the regiment was sent to serve overseas due to the outbreak of the War of the Spanish Succession, during which it was deployed in the Iberian Peninsula and fought at the bloody Battle of Almansa. In 1715, after coming back

Troopers of the 7th Dragoons (left) and the 3rd Dragoons (right).

home, it was made part of the British forces that were tasked with suppressing the Jacobite Rising. During the following decades, the regiment remained on garrison duty in southern England, where it was mostly employed to counteract smuggling. With the outbreak of the War of the Austrian Succession, the unit was sent to mainland Europe, where it took part in the Battle of Dettingen (1743) and Battle of Fontenoy (1745). During the Second Jacobite Rebellion, the regiment was rapidly sent back home and participated in the decisive Battle of Culloden that saw the defeat of the Jacobites. Until the outbreak of the Napoleonic Wars, the regiment saw little action apart from a few minor engagements fought against the French during the Seven Years' War.

Trooper of the 7th Dragoons.

Trooper of the 7th Dragoons. (*Royal Collection Trust / © His Majesty King Charles III 2024*)

4th Dragoons: raised in 1685 as Princess Anne of Denmark's Regiment of Dragoons, this unit joined William of Orange soon after the outbreak of the Glorious Revolution. It was sent to Scotland, where it fought against the Jacobites, and was later ordered to continental Europe to take part in the War of the Grand Alliance (seeing action on several occasions). During the War of the Spanish Succession, it was sent to the Iberian Peninsula and fought with determination at the bloody Battle of Almansa (1707). With the outbreak of the 1715 Jacobite Rising, it was employed against the Scottish insurgents and took part in the Battle of Sheriffmuir. After many years spent on garrison duty in Britain, the regiment returned to mainland Europe with the outbreak of the War of the Austrian Succession, fighting at the Battle of Dettingen (1743) and Battle of Lauffeld (1747). The corps did not see action during the Seven Years' War.

5th Dragoons: raised in 1689 as part of William of Orange's new English Army during the Glorious Revolution, it originally had the official denomination of Colonel Wynn's Regiment of Dragoons. In 1690, it participated in the Williamite Wars in Ireland, taking part in the Battle of the Boyne and the Battle of Aughrim (both fought in 1690). In 1704, the unit was renamed as the Royal Dragoons of Ireland, later being sent to continental Europe to fight in the War of the Spanish Succession. During the latter conflict, it participated in the following engagements: Blenheim (1704), Ramilies (1706), Oudenarde (1708) and Malplaquet (1709). During the following decades, the unit remained as part of the garrison in Ireland, where it was mostly tasked with patrolling the countryside and preventing the outbreak of local revolts.

6th Dragoons: raised in 1689 for William of Orange's new English Army during the Glorious Revolution, it had the original official denomination of Richard Cunningham's Regiment of Dragoons. However, the unit soon received the famous nickname of the Enniskilling Dragoons after it was quartered in Enniskilling Castle in northern Ireland. In 1690, it took part in the decisive Battle of the Boyne, later remaining in Ireland for some time. When the Jacobite Rising of 1715 began, the regiment was transferred to Scotland, where it fought against the Jacobites at the Battle of Sheriffmuir. With the outbreak of the War of the Austrian Secession it was transferred to continental Europe, participating in the following battles: Dettingen (1743), Fontenoy (1745), Rocoux (1746) and Lauffeld (1747). During the Seven Years' War, the corps was sent to fight against France and took part in the engagements at Minden and Wetter (1759).

Trooper of the 8th Dragoons. In 1748, the facing colour was changed from orange to yellow.

Trooper of the 8th Dragoons, with the new yellow facings. (*Royal Collection Trust / © His Majesty King Charles III 2024*)

7th Dragoons: raised in 1690 as part of the Scottish Army, during its expansion ordered by William of Orange after the Glorious Revolution, the regiment took part in the Grand Alliance War and the War of the Spanish Succession in continental Europe. It later fought in the Jacobite Rising of 1715, fighting at the Battle of Sheriffmuir. During the War of the Austrian Succession, it participated in the battles of Dettingen, Fontenoy, Rocoux and Lauffeld. In 1760, it took part in the Battle of Warburg during the Seven Years' War.

8th Dragoons: raised during 1693 in Ireland as a dragoon unit, it participated in the War of the Spanish Succession, suffering heavy losses. After having been

Trooper of the 9th Dragoons. (*Royal Collection Trust / © His Majesty King Charles III 2024*)

Troopers of the 9th Dragoons (left) and the 10th Dragoons (right).

completely reorganized, it took part in the crushing of the Jacobite Rising of 1715. The regiment returned to Scotland when the Jacobite Rising of 1745 began, helping to suppress the revolt. It did not see action during the Seven Years' War.

9th Dragoons: this unit was created during the Jacobite Rising of 1715 as part of the British military response to the Scottish revolt. It spent many years performing garrison duties in Ireland and did not serve overseas.

10th Dragoons: this regiment was created during the Jacobite Rising of 1715, part of the British military response to the Scottish rebellion. For twenty-five years, it remained on garrison duty in Cornwall until being despatched to Scotland in 1745 to fight against the Jacobites. During the Seven Years' War, it was sent for the first time to continental Europe, participating with distinction to the battles at Minden (1759) and Warburg (1760).

Trooper of the 11th Dragoons.

Farrier of the 11th Dragoons. (*Royal Collection Trust / © His Majesty King Charles III 2024*)

Troopers of the 12th Dragoons (left) and the 13th Dragoons (right).

11th Dragoons: this regiment was also created as a dragoon unit during the Jacobite Rising of 1715. It remained on garrison duty in Scotland for several years and participated to the crushing of the 1745 Jacobite Rising. In 1760, the regiment was despatched to Germany in order to take part in the Seven Years' War, fighting during that same year at the Battle of Warburg.

12th Dragoons: this regiment was formed as a dragoon unit during the Jacobite Rising of 1715. Three years later, it was placed on the Irish Establishment of the British Army and sent to Ireland in order to act as a garrison unit. It operated as such for seventy-five years.

13th Dragoons: raised during the military emergency caused by the Jacobite Rebellion of 1715, it was later despatched to Ireland, where it remained as part of the garrison until 1742. With the outbreak of the 1745 Jacobite Rising, it was sent to Scotland, where it suffered heavy casualties during a series of minor clashes fought against the rebel Highlanders. After the end of the revolt, the unit was sent back to Ireland, where it remained for several decades.

14th Dragoons: the regiment was raised during the Jacobite Rebellion of 1715, later being despatched to Ireland, where it remained on garrison duty until 1742. With the outbreak of the 1745 Jacobite Rising, it was sent to Scotland, suffering many losses in several minor clashes with the rebel Highlanders. At the end of the revolt, the regiment returned to Ireland, remaining there for several decades.

Chapter 8
Light Cavalry

During the first four decades of the eighteenth century, heavy cavalry was the most important component of European armies' mounted troops, since it made up the bulk of the cavalry forces mobilized by the various nations and had acquired tactical supremacy on the continent's battlefields. Highly trained and well-disciplined, it consisted of horsemen wielding long swords with a straight blade and mounted on massive horses, who were able to charge and manoeuvre in perfect order by maintaining knee-to-knee close formations. This kind of cavalry was mostly employed to conduct frontal charges and to cover the retreat of the line infantry when it was routed by the enemy. Since the Thirty Years' War, however, cavalry had started to perform a series of auxiliary roles for the infantry and was rarely used in an autonomous way. A perfect example of the kind of war that was fought in the eighteenth century was represented by the Prussian Army of Frederick the Great, which perfected close line infantry and heavy cavalry tactics and was admired by all the officer corps of Europe. Its soldiers were the best in Europe and their methods of training were copied by all armies, whether enemies or allies. During the War of the Austrian Succession (1740–1748) and the Seven Years' War (1756–1763), however, numerous episodes showed that the Prussian heavy cavalry was not as perfect as it may seem. It became apparent that it could experience serious problems while operating on broken terrain and when fighting against enemy units that employed hit-and-run guerrilla tactics. In particular, the Prussians struggled to counteract the efficient light troops deployed by the Austrian Empire, which consisted of semi-regular light cavalrymen recruited from Hungary. The light cavalry of the Austrian Army, commonly known as hussars, had been fighting for decades against the Ottoman Turks on the southern frontier of the Austrian Empire. The empire lived in a state of endless conflict, during which both sides launched numerous rapid incursions into the territory of the enemy to raid and pillage. Gradually, the Austrian border troops learned how to fight like their enemies, becoming expert in the art of skirmishing and scouting. Their usual area of operations was covered by mountains and woods, where each cavalryman had to move individually and not in close formation. These fighters were the direct heirs of a glorious military tradition, which had originated in Hungary during the late Renaissance: the hussars were the Hungarian national cavalry, like the

Troopers of the light troop attached to the 11th Dragoons in 1757.

Drummer (left) and trooper (right) of the 15th Light Dragoons.

uhlans (lancers) were for the Polish. Most of the Hungarian light horsemen were farmers in their civilian life and lived on the Balkan frontier as military settlers, their innovative tactics being derived from direct combat experience and based on the principle of 'open formation'. According to such tactics, each cavalryman advanced autonomously but always maintained contact with the other members of his unit, allowing him to cover his advance behind obstacles on the terrain (like a tree, for example) and fire upon the enemy from a favourable position. With these tactics, firearms also became important for cavalry and started playing a prominent role on the battlefield. During the War of the Austrian Succession, on several occasions, the Hungarian light cavalrymen of the Austrian Army caused serious troubles and losses to Frederick the Great's heavy mounted troops. Initially, they were considered as simple 'murderers' by the most traditionalist of their enemies, but over time it became apparent that they could play a very important tactical role. The other great powers of Europe, differently from Austria, had no militarized border from which expert light mounted fighters could be recruited, so they started to create their own light cavalry formations by recruiting Hungarian mercenaries or prisoners of war. This was the case with France and several other European nations, where hussar units proliferated during the middle of the eighteenth century. The new light horsemen of the European armies adopted the same uniforms and weapons as the Hungarian hussars, but various local versions of them soon started to appear. In some countries, including Great Britain, the new light cavalry assumed from the beginning various distinctive features and were quite different from those of Austria or France.

The general expansion of the light cavalry units continued well after the end of the War of the Austrian Succession, the combat experiences of the following Seven Years' War doing nothing but confirm the tactical importance of the new light formations. A new form of warfare was born, the *petite guerre* or little war, which was based on low intensity combat and hit-and-run tactics. The British Army was greatly affected by the light cavalry revolution that took place in the eighteenth century, its cavalry starting to be modernized during the crucial years that saw the end of the War of the Austrian Succession and the outbreak of the Jacobite Rising (1745–1748). It should be noted, however, that in Great Britain the introduction of new light cavalry tactics encountered very strong opposition: the British officer corps of the time, especially that of the cavalry, was an extremely conservative one that considered with suspicion any innovation coming from abroad. Over time, however, evidence obliged the traditionalists to abandon their positions. Until 1745, the British Army comprised only heavy cavalry units (horse regiments) and medium cavalry units (dragoon regiments). In that year, however, the Second Jacobite Rising began in Scotland, during which the British cavalry experienced serious difficulties in chasing down the highly mobile insurgent forces of the Highlanders, who moved rapidly on the broken terrain of northern Scotland and were masters in employing hit-and-run tactics. As a consequence, the Duke of Kingston, one of the English nobles who supported the British military efforts against the Jacobites, decided to raise a volunteer horse regiment with light cavalry training from his land possessions in Nottinghamshire. This new corps, organized by the duke at his own expense, was officially ranked as a regiment of horse but its members were trained as light cavalrymen, despite being equipped and uniformed like standard heavy horsemen. The Duke of Kingston's Regiment of Horse performed extremely well during the Jacobite Rebellion and fought at the decisive Battle of Culloden, after which it pursued the defeated Jacobites with great determination. Initially, the regulars of the British Army held many prejudices against this new light corps, but combat experience showed them the potential of such units. After the end of the Jacobite Rising, in 1746, the experimental volunteer regiment raised by the Duke of Kingston was disbanded, its members having been enlisted only for the duration of the war. The Duke of Cumberland, who had commanded the British Army at Culloden, had a very positive opinion of the unit and would have preferred to retain it in service. Although this was not possible for practical reasons, Cumberland found a way to maintain some light cavalry in his forces, organizing a new light cavalry unit, known as the Duke of Cumberland's Regiment of Light Dragoons, in which he enlisted all the men of the recently disbanded Duke of Kingston's Regiment of Horse. The new corps was the first regular light cavalry unit ever formed in the history of the British Army, as well as the first to be ranked as Light Dragoons. The regiment was soon dispatched to continental Europe and participated to the final operations of the War of the Austrian Succession, distinguishing itself at the Battle of Lauffeld. In 1749, however, the Duke of Cumberland's Regiment of Light Dragoons was disbanded soon after the end of hostilities in Europe. The Duke of Cumberland was one of the first British officers to understand the importance and potential of the new light cavalry corps. During the Second Jacobite Uprising, for example, he had a small personal bodyguard formed by a few hussars who were recruited in Hungary. These, despite being just a handful of men, fought with distinction at Culloden and made a good impression to the most traditionalist officers of the British Army. The Duke of Cumberland's Hussars were the first unit of the British Army to wear the traditional dress of the Hungarian light cavalry. Until 1757, the British cavalry continued to be made up only of horse regiments and dragoon regiments, the experimental cavalry corps active from 1745–1749 no longer being in existence. It was only a matter of time, however, before Britain became involved into another European conflict, with the Seven Years' War breaking out, during which the need for new light cavalry units soon became increasingly strong in all the major armies of the time, the British Army being no exception to this rule.

In April 1757, the formation of a total of eleven independent troops of light cavalry was authorized, each of which was attached to one of the existing cavalry regiments and had the following internal establishment: three officers, one troop quartermaster, five NCOs, two drummers and sixty troopers. Members of these new troops were

Drummer of the 15th Light Dragoons. (*Royal Collection Trust / © His Majesty King Charles III 2024*)

Trooper of the 16th Light Dragoons.

chosen from the youngest and fittest recruits of the existing cavalry regiments. They were mounted on small and nimble horses, and were trained to act as skirmishers and explorers. The new light horsemen continued to wear the standard uniforms of their parent regiments, but received a distinctive headgear: a black leather helmet with an upright comb, a frontal plate mounted with brass and a drooping feather. They were still armed with straight-bladed swords, but also carried a flintlock carbine and a couple of pistols. The glorious tradition of the British Light Dragoons was thus born. Within a few years, the new light troops showed all their great potential, to the point that in 1759 it was decided to form seven independent regiments of light cavalry. These were recruited very rapidly and were numbered in progressive order after the fourteen regiments of dragoons that already existed at the time. The following new units of Light Dragoons were organized:

15th Regiment of Light Dragoons: raised in the London area by George Augustus Eliott, it soon distinguished itself during the Battle of Emsdorf (1760) that was fought in Germany. After also taking part in the Battle of Wilhelmsthal (1762), it returned home.

16th Regiment of Light Dragoons: this unit, raised by John Burgoyne, took part in the final operations of the Seven Years' War.

Trooper of the 16th Light Dragoons. (*Royal Collection Trust / © His Majesty King Charles III 2024*)

Trooper of the 17th Light Dragoons.

17th Regiment of Light Dragoons: raised in Scotland, it was disbanded at the end of the Seven Years' War.

18th Regiment of Light Dragoons: this unit saw some action in Germany during 1761.

19th Regiment of Light Dragoons: saw no action during the Seven Years' War.

20th Regiment of Light Dragoons: raised in Ireland, it was disbanded at the end of the Seven Years' War.

21st Regiment of Light Dragoons: raised in England, it was disbanded at the end of the Seven Years' War. It was formed by assembling together some of the light cavalry troops that had been created in 1757.

By 1765, the British cavalry included a total of four regiments of Light Dragoons, which were augmented to five in 1768 when the 12th Regiment of Dragoons was transformed into a light unit. The internal organization of the regiments of Light Dragoons was the same as the horse and dragoons units. Each regiment was structured on six troops (sometimes supplemented by an additional seventh depot troop, for recruitment purposes). Each troop comprised the following elements: one captain, one lieutenant, one cornet, three sergeants, three corporals, two drummers, one hautboy and fifty-nine troopers. The three senior troops were commanded by the field officers of each regiment: a colonel, lieutenant colonel and major. On most occasions, however, as was the case in other formations of the British Army, the senior troop of a regiment was commanded by a captain lieutenant rather than the colonel.

Chapter 9

Royal Artillery, Royal Engineers and Marines

Until the beginning of the eighteenth century, the artillerymen of most European armies were required to fire their guns but were not equipped to defend themselves from enemy attacks; as a result, while on the battlefield, they had to be escorted by infantrymen specifically charged to do so. Until 1716, with the creation of the Royal Artillery, the British Army did not comprise any permanent company or battery of artillery, temporary artillery trains being organized by the Ordnance Department only when needed, usually being disbanded at the end of each campaign. At times of peace, several dozen professional gunners were at the service of the Ordnance Department, scattered across Britain and manning the guns of the various garrisons. During wartime, they were assembled to form a train and were supplemented with a number of mattrosses (gunner's assistants) and pioneers, who were semi-skilled civilian labourers contracted only for the duration of a campaign. The conductors of the carts that were used to move the artillery pieces were also all civilians. Consequently, the eighteenth century was a period of great change and progressive professionalization for the British artillery. The first two permanent companies/batteries of artillery of the British Army were established in 1716, receiving the official denomination of Royal Artillery in 1720, although in practice they were an autonomous military force from their creation. The two original companies were rapidly increased to four and were assembled – at least from an administrative point of view – with the artillery companies that were part of the garrison in Gibraltar and Menorca since the end of the War of the Spanish Succession. As a result of these organizational changes, in 1722 it was possible to create the Royal Regiment of Artillery. This had the numerical consistency of a single battalion, but its members soon became famous for their great skill and professionalism. From the onset, selection and promotion in the ranks of the Royal Artillery were based on merit, meaning the officer corps of this new branch of service comprised only excellent elements. In 1741, in order to improve the general quality of all the artillerymen serving across the British Empire, a cadet company was formed at the Royal Military Academy in Woolwich, tasked with training not only officers of the Royal Artillery Regiment but also those serving with the British East India Company. In 1757, the Royal Artillery Regiment was reorganized into two battalions with twelve companies each, its expansion continuing during the following decades. By 1775, it comprised the following sub-units: four active battalions with ten companies each, two independent companies made up of veteran invalids (performing garrison duties) and a permanent military band. The various battalions of the Royal Artillery Regiment were not employed on the field as complete units, their companies/batteries usually being deployed as autonomous corps. When this happened, they were commonly known as brigades despite consisting of companies with just six pieces each. Attached to each brigade was a detachment of civilian artillery drivers, which was tasked with moving the guns on the battlefield. Ireland had an independent artillery corps known as the Royal Irish Artillery, which was formed in 1755 and was mostly tasked with providing drafts for the Royal Artillery Regiment as well as some units of garrison artillery. The standard establishment of a Royal Artillery company/battery/brigade comprised the following elements: two captains, two first lieutenants, one second lieutenant, four sergeants, four corporals, 100 gunners and three drummers. Of the six artillery pieces that were manned by a company/battery/brigade, on most occasions five were field guns and one was a howitzer. These were transported together with their limbers and various wagons that were essential for their functioning: ammunition-wagons, baggage-wagons and spare-wheel wagons. In addition, each artillery brigade had a field forge that was vital for repairing damaged pieces. A total of about 100 drivers and 200 draught animals were usually needed to move a single artillery battery.

The Corps of Royal Engineers, like the Royal Artillery, was organized as a permanent military unit only in 1716. Until then, the British Army had included only a few independent officers with specific engineering skills. The formation of an independent Corps of Engineers (the 'Royal' prefix was added in 1787), however, did not change the existing situation in a significant way: until the outbreak of the Napoleonic Wars, the British Engineers continued to comprise just a few commissioned officers who had undergone some specific technical training at Woolwich. Like the Royal Artillery, the Royal Engineers were not under the direct administrative control of the British Army, as they were managed by the efficient Board of Ordnance. Their officers, like those of the artillery, were promoted according to seniority and merit, differently from officers of the army (who purchased their commissions). The labour force for the Royal Engineers was provided by the pioneers of the various infantry regiments. A single company of Royal Military Artificers was created only in 1772, but this was always deployed in Gibraltar until 1783.

The long history of the English (later British) naval infantry began on 28 October 1664, when Charles II ordered the creation of a naval infantry regiment to fight against the Netherlands in the Second Anglo-Dutch War. The new unit had the

Officer of the Royal Artillery Regiment in 1740.

Gunner of the Royal Artillery Regiment in 1750.

official denomination of the Duke of York and Albany's Maritime Regiment of Foot, but it soon became known as the Admiral's Regiment. The corps mustered 1,200 soldiers assembled into six companies, who were mostly recruited from the Trained Bands of London (the efficient militia of the English capital). At that time, future monarch James II was both the Duke of York and Albany and the Lord High Admiral, so the new regiment placed under his command had an elite status from its foundation (it wore, for example, a distinctive yellow uniform). Shortly after the creation of the Admiral's Regiment, another naval infantry unit was created: the Holland Regiment, which was later transformed into a standard infantry regiment as the 3rd Foot (The Buffs). Both the Admiral's Regiment and the Holland Regiment were paid for by the Treasurer of the Navy. Following the Glorious Revolution, William of Orange ordered the disbandment of the Admiral's Regiment and the transformation of the Holland Regiment into a standard infantry corps. In 1690, two new naval infantry regiments were raised: the Earl of Pembroke's Maritime Regiment and Lord Berkeley's Maritime Regiment. These were merged into a single unit in 1698, when three of the existing regiments of foot were transformed into naval infantry. In 1699, however, all four naval infantry units were disbanded. A few years later, in 1702, six new regiments of naval infantry (now defined as 'marines') were raised for service in the War of the Spanish Succession. At the same time, six new line infantry regiments tasked with

Officer of the Royal Artillery Regiment in 1770.

Officer of the Royal Engineers in 1755.

Privates of the 1st Marines (left) and the 2nd Marines (right).

Privates of the 3rd Marines (left) and the 4th Marines (right).

Privates of the 5th Marines (left) and the 6th Marines (right).

Privates of the 7th Marines (left) and the 8th Marines (right).

Privates of the 9th Marines (left) and the 10th Marines (right).

serving on warships were also created (these were known as Sea Service Regiments). The twelve new units created in 1702 performed very well during the War of the Spanish Succession, capturing Gibraltar from the Spaniards and defending it against superior enemy forces. When hostilities came to an end, three of the naval infantry regiments were disbanded and three were transformed into line units (31st, 32nd and 33rd Foot). The Sea Service Regiments, meanwhile, went back to their usual functions of standard line infantry.

The combat experience gained in the War of the Spanish Succession had proved to the British military authorities that a strong corps of naval infantry was absolutely vital if Britain wanted to expand its colonial possessions around the world. Future confrontations with France and Spain would take place far from Europe and have a distinct naval nature. In 1739, shortly before the outbreak of the War of the Austrian Succession, hostilities broke out between Great Britain and Spain in what became known as the War of Jenkin's Ear. This conflict was mostly fought in the Caribbean, where the British attacked several of the flourishing Spanish colonies. Since this war was fought mostly at sea, the British government decided to raise six new regiments of Marines in 1739, following the example of those created in 1702. The new units were soon followed by another four, bringing the total number of naval infantry regiments to ten; these were numbered as the 1st–10th Marines, but were also included in the list of the line infantry units as the 44th–53rd Regiments of Foot. An additional naval infantry regiment was raised from the colonists of North America, to attack the Spanish stronghold of Cartagena in present-day Colombia. This unit, known as Gooch's American Regiment, had a large establishment, with thirty-six companies assembled into four battalions. Each of the Thirteen Colonies contributed to its formation by recruiting a number of companies: eight from Pennsylvania, five each from Massachusetts and New York, four each from Virginia and North Carolina, three each from New Jersey and Maryland, and two each from Rhode Island and Connecticut. Gooch's American Regiment was almost destroyed during the British expedition against Cartagena, which was one of the worst British military disasters during the War of the Austrian Succession; it was disbanded in 1742. The ten regiments of Marines formed in Great Britain served with distinction during the War of the Austrian Succession, being disbanded only after the conflict came to an end in 1748. In 1755, following the outbreak of the Seven Years' War, the British government finally decided to organize an independent and permanent corps of naval infantry, which received the official denomination of Marines (the latter was changed to Royal Marines only in 1802). The new naval infantrymen were initially structured on fifteen autonomous companies, each of which could be sent to serve on one warship; differently from the sailors of the Royal Navy, the

Officer (left) and privates (right) of the Marines in 1755.

Marines were all volunteers, like the infantrymen of the army, and thus had a lot in common with the latter (including their red uniform). The various companies of Marines were assembled, administratively, into three divisions that took their name from the location where they were based: Chatham, Portsmouth and Plymouth.

Each company of Marines comprised the following elements: one captain, two first lieutenants, two second lieutenants, eight sergeants, eight corporals, five drummers and 130 privates. The main tasks of the Marines – which were part of the navy, not the army – were the following: acting as marksmen on warships, conducting boarding operations, manning the guns of the warships on which they served and organizing amphibious landings. In addition, they had to prevent or crush mutinies that might take place among the sailors of a warship. The great success achieved by the new naval infantrymen during the Seven Years' War guaranteed a long existence for their corps.

Chapter 10

Auxiliary Corps and Allied Contingents

The outbreak of the Jacobite Rising in 1745 found the British Army with its best units fighting on the Continent against France, which caused serious problems to the British government. In order to counter the Highlanders' rebellion before it could threaten the city of London, the authorities had to raise new auxiliary corps on their home territory that could support the few available regular units in Britain. The uprising of 1745 was thus a genuine military emergency, which obliged the British Army to employ all the resources that it could mobilize. Soon after the outbreak of the rebellion, various leading aristocrats enthusiastically offered to raise and maintain volunteer military corps. A total of fifteen of these 'Noblemen's Regiments' were created: thirteen regiments of foot and two regiments of horse. The infantry units were mostly employed as garrison troops (several of them never left their home towns) or to guard rebel prisoners; their real purpose was to demonstrate the patriotic credentials of their creators, who soon realized they lacked the necessary financial resources to fund their new military units. The various Noblemen's Regiments thus started to be paid by the government, which was never particularly happy about their effectiveness and thus disbanded them as soon as possible. The only unit that distinguished itself on the field of battle was the Duke of Kingston's Horse, one of the two cavalry regiments; thanks to its light cavalry training, it played an important role in the operations that led to the defeat of the Jacobites. During the Jacobite Rising of 1745, the British regulars were also supported by smaller volunteer units, not raised by major aristocrats but by gentlemen with strong patriotic feelings. These formations – which usually consisted of single infantry or cavalry companies – performed a series of auxiliary functions, such as assisting with the transportation of supplies or arresting those suspected of plotting with the Jacobites. By freeing the regulars from these second-line duties, they made a significant contribution to the British cause. Among the most important volunteer units of this kind were the Loyal Blue Fusiliers, the Liverpool Blues, the Yorkshire Blues and the Yorkshire Hunters. Volunteer corps loyal to the Crown were also formed in Scotland. The first to be created, on 9 September 1745, was the Edinburgh Regiment, which was soon expanded to become a brigade after incorporating volunteers from other areas of Scotland. The Edinburgh Regiment was quickly followed by the Glasgow

Regiment, which had a semi-regular status like the unit raised in the Scottish capital. The few clans that remained loyal to George II contributed to the British war effort by mobilizing their own militias, 18 semi-regular independent Highland Companies being formed, which supplemented the 18 regular companies created by the government for the anti-partisan operations that followed the Battle of Culloden. The auxiliary corps in British service during the Jacobite Rising of 1745 also included a volunteer unit that had been raised for service in North America by Brigadier General James Oglethorpe, who was the governor of Georgia (one of the Thirteen Colonies). This formation, the Georgia Rangers, had just been established and was on the verge of being sent to the Americas when the Jacobite Rising began, but the government decided to employ it against the Highlanders instead. The Georgia Rangers, which already had one company of Highland infantry in North America, consisted of two mounted troops that were to have been tasked with patrolling the coastline of Georgia. Each troop comprised one captain, two lieutenants, one cornet, four quartermasters, two hornists and sixty privates. Brigaded with the Yorkshire Hunters, the Georgia Rangers participated in several minor engagements and were without doubt the most exotic unit of the British military forces, due to their green uniforms designed for use in the American woodlands and the presence of some Creek natives among their ranks. All the volunteer corps described above, despite their different natures, were rapidly disbanded after the end of the rebellion.

During the Jacobite Rising of 1745 the British Army, could also call upon the professional military contingents provided by two allied states: the United Provinces of the Netherlands and Hesse-Kassel. The Dutch auxiliary contingent was provided under a treaty of mutual assistance that had been signed between Great Britain and the United Provinces some years before, according to which each of the two countries was to aid the other one in case they were threatened by a foreign invasion. The forces sent by the Dutch to Great Britain in 1745 consisted of six infantry regiments: those of Braekel, Holstein-Gottorp, Tissot van Patot, Villattes, La Rocque and Hirtzel. The first five of these units were made up of Dutch soldiers, while the last one was a Swiss mercenary regiment (at that time the Dutch Army included several units of German and Swiss mercenaries). The five Dutch regiments had two battalions each, while the single Swiss regiment had three battalions. The Dutch expeditionary force included a small artillery detachment, but no cavalry. The Dutch units never saw action and had a very difficult relationship with the British population, being accused of robbery, riot and affray on several occasions. The Dutch soldiers left Britain a few months after their arrival and were replaced by an expeditionary force provided by the German state of Hesse-Kassel. Leasing military units to foreign powers like Britain or the Netherlands was an important source of income for several

Grenadiers from different regiments of the Dutch infantry, from left to right: Hirtzel, Constant and Stuerier. The Hirtzel Regiment, a mercenary Swiss unit, was part of the Dutch expeditionary force deployed in Great Britain during 1745. (*Royal Collection Trust / © His Majesty King Charles III 2024*)

German princedoms during the eighteenth century. The Landgraviate of Hesse-Kassel, for example, rented out part of its professional military forces several times, a practice that allowed the rulers of the state to maintain a large standing army for many decades (which was difficult to achieve financially). The leasing of professional units took place according to the Subsidy System, which was introduced by William of Orange in 1672 for the Dutch Army. This was based on rental contracts signed between the Netherlands and other states, according to which the Dutch paid a rental fee to the German princedoms, the wages of the troops that had been hired and provided the latter with all necessary supplies. In exchange for this, the German princedoms had to keep the hired units up to strength by sending a sufficient number of new recruits, but were freed (albeit temporarily) from the high costs of maintaining a standing army. The Subsidy System was soon adopted by Britain, which used it

Hanoverian grenadier of the Fussgarde Regiment.

Grenadiers from different regiments of the Hanoverian infantry, from left to right: Block, Hattorf and Hammerstein. (*Royal Collection Trust / © His Majesty King Charles III 2024*)

during the Jacobite Rising to hire the Hesse-Kassel contingent. This consisted of six infantry units – the Garde, Prinz Maximilian, Mansbach, Von Donop, Erbprinz and Grenadiere regiments – plus a single squadron of hussars. The whole force was hired at a cost of 100,000 crowns and comprised 5,000 soldiers. The Garde Regiment was the best of the Hessian infantry, as it was the guard unit of the German state, while the Grenadiere Regiment was a chosen corps, its companies all being grenadier ones. Like their Dutch predecessors, despite being well disciplined, the Hessians saw no action during the Jacobite Rising before leaving Britain in May 1746.

After the outbreak of the Seven Years' War, Britain assembled an army in western Germany to support Frederick the Great – Britain's only ally in the ongoing conflict – in his struggle against France and Austria. This force, known as His Britannic Majesty's Army in Germany, was paid by the British and was mostly tasked with protecting Hanover. At that time, Hanover was a possession of the British monarch

Grenadiers from different regiments of the Hanoverian infantry, from left to right: Alt-Zastrow, Diepenbroick and Hausz. (*Royal Collection Trust / © His Majesty King Charles III 2024*)

George II, whose family came from the German state, so Great Britain and the German princedom were ruled by the same monarch in 'personal union'. France had long wanted to invade Hanover, having attempted to do so in the past, so in order to have a strong ally on the Continent that could protect Hanoverian territory, the British government formed an alliance with Frederick of Prussia. The army assembled by Britain in western Germany consisted of contingents from several different states: a British expeditionary force, the Hanoverian Army (supported by a small subsidiary contingent from the neighbouring state of Buckenburg, paid by Hanover), the army of Hesse-Kassel and the army of Brunswick. The latter German princedoms had been allies of Great Britain for several years and had already provided troops to the British government under the Subsidy System during the War of the Austrian Succession. After the Seven Years' War, they continued to be allies of the British and provided significant military contingents to them during the American Revolution

Grenadiers from different regiments of the Hanoverian infantry, from left to right: Oberg, Ledebour and Hardenberg. (*Royal Collection Trust / © His Majesty King Charles III 2024*)

of 1775–1783. What follows are brief details on the organization and uniforms of military units for each of the German states that contributed to the formation of His Britannic Majesty's Army in Germany.

Hanover: the Hanoverian Army, despite wearing red uniforms that were quite similar to those of the British Army, had very little in common with them. Among the military forces of the German princedoms, it was one of the largest and most experienced armies, having fought against the French on several occasions. In 1756, the infantry of the Hanoverian Army consisted of twenty-seven battalion-sized regiments: twenty-four of musketeers and three of grenadiers. Each regiment contained seven companies of 122 officers and men each, each musketeer company – albeit only administratively – including eight grenadiers, who were detached to provide the personnel for the formation of a composite grenadier company. The various composite grenadier companies were assembled into the three regiments of

Hanoverian trooper of the Grenadieren zu Pferde Regiment.

grenadiers, which had elite status. The infantry of the Hanoverian Army also included one guard regiment, known as the Fussgarde. This had a large establishment of two battalions, and its grenadiers were not detached from their parent companies (since they were tasked with bodyguard duties). Each Hanoverian infantry regiment had a staff of nineteen officers and NCOs, except for the Fussgarde, which had a twenty-strong staff. In 1758, another two musketeer regiments, with only five companies

Hanoverian trooper from the mounted grenadier company of the Pontpietin Dragoon Regiment. (*Royal Collection Trust / © His Majesty King Charles III 2024*)

The uniforms of the Hanoverian Jager Corps, from left to right: mounted jager, foot jager and grenadier.

each and without grenadiers, were added. The cavalry of the Hanoverian Army consisted of eight cuirassier regiments and four dragoon regiments. The cuirassier units had six companies each, which were assembled into two squadrons; a single squadron mustered 361 officers and men. One of the cuirassier regiments had guard status and was known as the Leib-Regiment, or Bodyguard Regiment. The dragoon regiments were considerably larger than the cuirassier units, each of them having eight companies assembled into four squadrons. One of the dragoon regiments had guard status and was known as Grenadieren zu Pferde, or Horse Grenadiers, despite being a dragoon unit. Like the Prussian Army, that of Hanover included light infantry and light cavalry units belonging to two main categories: the regular light corps and Freikorps (mercenaries). At the beginning of the Seven Years' War, the Hanoverian regular troops had no light units, but in May 1757 a Jager Corps was raised, consisting of just two companies. One company was of foot jagers and the

Carabinier of the Scheither Freikorps (left) and trooper of Luckner's Hussars (right). Both units were in Hanoverian service.

other of mounted jagers. The Hanoverian jagers were expanded with the addition of two foot companies in 1758, followed by another mounted company in 1759. The regular light infantrymen distinguished themselves on several occasions, especially after the Jager Corps came under the orders of Colonel Freytag, so it was expanded to comprise six foot companies and six mounted companies. In 1762, the Jager Corps

Grenadiers from different regiments of the Hesse-Kassel infantry, from left to right: Stammer, Tunderfeld and Both. (*Royal Collection Trust / © His Majesty King Charles III 2024*)

was consolidated as a single battalion with four companies, after having absorbed a Freikorps – known as Stockhausen's Jagers – consisting of one grenadier company and four jager companies (two on foot and two mounted). The first Freikorps to enter Hanoverian service was a small detachment of hussars – Luckner's Hussars – that had previously been in Dutch service. Expanded to two companies in 1758, the hussars had the opportunity to show their valour as skirmishers and explorers, and by 1760 they consisted of eight companies assembled into four squadrons. In May 1758, a new Freikorps was raised for Hanoverian service by Captain Scheither. This initially comprised a single company, but by 1761 it had been expanded to comprise the following: two companies of grenadiers, one company of jagers, four companies of carabiniers (heavy cavalry) and one detachment of artillery. At the beginning of the Seven Years' War, the Hanoverian Army's artillery consisted of six companies, each with sixty-seven officers and men, but these were soon reorganized into four field

Hesse-Kassel grenadier of the Graf von Hessenstein Infantry Regiment.

Officers of the Hesse-Kassel Leib Infantry Regiment in parade dress (left) and campaign dress (right). (*Colour plate by Herbert Knotel, part of the Anne S.K. Brown Military Collection*)

artillery brigades with two or three companies apiece. Attached to the Hanoverian Army there was a small subsidiary contingent provided by the state of Buckenburg, which comprised one infantry regiment, one jager company, one carabinier company and one artillery company. In December 1759, in support of the war efforts of its ally Frederick the Great, Britain decided to fund the raising of some Freikorps in Hanover. The Hanoverian Army was ordered to provide the cadres for these new Freikorps, which later became collectively known as the Légion Britannique; these consisted of forty officers and eighty NCOs who, thanks to their experience, were

NCO (left) and standard-bearer (right) of the Hesse-Kassel Leib Infantry Regiment. (*Colour plate by Herbert Knotel, part of the Anne S.K. Brown Military Collection*)

able to effectively train the new corps. By the beginning of April 1760, five battalions of infantry and five squadrons of dragoons had been formed. Each foot battalion consisted of four musketeer companies, while the dragoon squadrons included sizeable numbers of experienced troopers detached from the Hanoverian Army's cavalry regiments. The Légion Britannique was in British pay and served alongside Hanoverian forces. Later, each of its infantry battalions was given two 3-pdr guns. As the Freikorps was mostly recruited from deserters and prisoners of war, it suffered from high rates of desertion from the beginning.

Hesse-Kassel: the Landgraviate of Hesse-Kassel, located in western Germany south of Hanover, had one of the best and largest professional armies of the Holy Roman Empire. In terms of quality and numbers in Germany, the troops of Hesse-Kassel were inferior only to those of the four major states (Austria, Prussia, Bavaria and Saxony). At the beginning of the Seven Years' War, the Hesse-Kassel infantry

Grenadier (left) and pioneer (right) of the Hesse-Kassel Leib Infantry Regiment. (*Colour plate by Herbert Knotel, part of the Anne S.K. Brown Military Collection*)

consisted of twelve battalion-sized regiments (eleven of musketeers and one of grenadiers), each of which had ten companies. In 1760, the ten companies of each musketeer unit were consolidated into eight, and were assembled into two battalions with four companies each. At the same time, the practice of drawing eight men from each musketeer company to serve as grenadiers ceased and the two remaining companies from each musketeer regiment were consolidated to form six independent grenadier battalions. In 1756, just one of the infantry regiments had guard status, the Leibgardezu Fuss. In 1760, however, a new guard infantry regiment was raised and the single grenadier regiment was given guard status. Following these organizational changes, the new guard infantry regiment formed in 1760 became the 1st Garde,

Musketeers of the Hesse-Kassel Leib Infantry Regiment in parade dress (left) and campaign dress (right). (*Colour plate by Herbert Knotel, part of the Anne S.K. Brown Military Collection*)

the grenadier regiment the 2nd Garde and the Leibgardezu Fuss the 3rd Garde. The 1st Garde had just one battalion, but the 2nd Garde and 3rd Garde each had two. After these changes, one line infantry regiment was elevated to guard status and became the 4th Garde (also known as the Leib-Regiment). Two of the remaining line infantry regiments were later transformed from musketeer into fusilier units, but this had little practical consequence. As a result of the above, the Hesse-Kassel infantry consisted of the following units in 1763: four Guard regiments, seven musketeer regiments and two fusilier regiments. The Hesse-Kassel cavalry included both horse and dragoon regiments. The horse regiments were heavy cavalry units of cuirassiers, but were not equipped with metal cuirasses. There were four horse regiments, each with two squadrons, while the two dragoon regiments had four squadrons apiece. In 1760, as part of the general reorganization of the Hesse-Kassel military that took place in that year, a small Garde du Corps mounted bodyguard was formed and added to the cavalry establishment, but this new unit performed only ceremonial duties. In addition to the cuirassiers and dragoons described above, the Hesse-Kassel

Trooper of the Hesse-Kassel dragoons.

Officer (left) and standard-bearer (right) of the Brunswick von Rhetz Infantry Regiments. (*Colour plate by Herbert Knotel, part of the Anne S.K. Brown Military Collection*)

cavalry also had a regiment of hussars. This had a quite peculiar history, having been formed in 1745 when Hesse-Kassel leased some of its military units to Britain in order to fight in Scotland during the Jacobite Rising. The unit was created as a single squadron with two companies, but in 1756 it was expanded to two squadrons. Under the reorganization of 1760, the Husaren-Korps came to comprise four squadrons. The Hesse-Kassel regular light troops consisted of a small Jager Corps with two foot companies, which from August 1759 were supplemented by two mounted companies. A single Freikorps was raised by Hesse-Kassel during the Seven Years' War, this being a light infantry battalion known as Chasseur Battalion von Rall. The Hesse-Kassel artillery had just two companies in 1756, but this increased to three in 1757 and five in 1760. These were responsible for the heavy pieces only, since the battalion guns of the infantry units were manned by a few gunners attached to the foot regiments. By the end of the Seven Years' War, the battalion guns were manned by four autonomous artillery companies. The Hesse-Kassel regular forces were supported by a territorial

Standard-bearer of the Brunswick Specht Infantry Regiment. (*Colour plate by Herbert Knotel, part of the Anne S.K. Brown Military Collection*)

Standard-bearer of the Brunswick Prinz Friedrich Infantry Regiment. (*Colour plate by Herbert Knotel, part of the Anne S.K. Brown Military Collection*)

Officer (left) and jager (right) of the Brunswick Light Infantry Battalion von Barner. (*Colour plate by Herbert Knotel, part of the Anne S.K. Brown Military Collection*)

militia known as the Landmiliz, which was mostly tasked with performing garrison and police duties. The militia was originally organized in three infantry regiments, but in 1760 these were transformed into one Garrison Grenadier Battalion and three Garrison Battalions (all with four companies each).

Brunswick: the small state of Brunswick, located in the heart of central Germany, was a loyal ally of both Great Britain and Prussia well before the outbreak of the Seven Years' War. It had small but efficient military forces, with significant combat experience. The Brunswick infantry consisted of four battalion-sized regiments, each of which had five musketeer companies and one grenadier company. The grenadier companies of each unit, during times of war, were usually detached from their

Officer of the Brunswick dragoons. (*Colour plate by Herbert Knotel, part of the Anne S.K. Brown Military Collection*)

Private of the Brunswick jagers. (*Colour plate by Herbert Knotel, part of the Anne S.K. Brown Military Collection*)

parent regiments to form two provisional grenadier battalions with two companies each. In 1759, the two grenadier battalions were expanded to three and became a permanent corps, independent from the line infantry. The Brunswick infantry was also enlarged in 1759 with the formation of two new battalions: an elite unit having guard status (the Leib-Grenadiere Garde) and a fusilier formation, which performed garrison duties (the Fusilier-Bataillon von Volschen). The Brunswick cavalry of 1756 consisted of a single unit, a dragoon regiment with four companies. In 1759, this was converted into a carabinier regiment and expanded to six companies assembled into three squadrons. The Brunswick cavalry was expanded during the same year with the formation of a new hussar regiment, which had four companies, increasing to six in 1761. The unit was raised with British funds but became an important component of the Brunswick Army. Until 1759, Brunswick had no regular light units, but in that year a small Jager Corps was formed, comprising three foot companies and two mounted companies. In 1762, it was expanded with the addition of a foot company and a mounted company. The corps also had two light artillery pieces, manned by thirteen gunners. A new light infantry battalion, known as Light Infantry Battalion von Barner, was raised in 1762. The first Freikorps in Brunswick service was also raised in 1762; this, known as the Volontaires Auxiliares de Bronswick, comprised three companies of grenadiers and three of cavalry (one of mounted grenadiers, one of hussars and one of *Bosniaken*, or lancers). It was mostly recruited from Balkan deserters or prisoners of war from the Austrian Army. The Brunswick artillery consisted of just three companies during the Seven Years' War.

Chapter 11

The British Military Forces in the Americas

Until the outbreak of the French-Indian War in 1754, the British military presence in North America was extremely limited from a numerical point of view: at the beginning of the eighteenth century, for example, there were only four independent companies of infantry stationed in New York, the members of which were all recruited from the local community and did not come from Britain. The scarcity of British regulars in the American colonies was the result of several different factors. First of all, the British government had never considered the colonies as important overseas territories. In comparison, India was much more flourishing than the American colonies from an economic point of view during the eighteenth century, so the British had no interest in spending large sums of money to garrison North America. In addition, it is important to bear in mind that most of the American colonies had a difficult relationship with the motherland. Those of New England, Massachusetts in particular, had been created by Puritan communities who had abandoned 'Old England' in order to live according to their religious beliefs. In their motherland they were persecuted by the Church of England as dissenters and were treated as potentially dangerous religious extremists, so in order to follow the moral laws contained in the Holy Bible and to avoid persecution, thousands of Puritans had migrated to North America during the seventeenth century. They lived very independently in their new homeland, practicing commerce and agriculture with excellent results. They no longer considered themselves as subjects of the English crown, so had no intention of paying heavy taxes or accept the presence of royalist garrisons on their territories. During the English Civil War, the colonies of New England supported the Parliamentary cause and later Cromwell's Commonwealth; as a result, when the monarchy was restored in England in 1660, they found themselves in a difficult political position. During the following decades they resisted all attempts made by the monarchy to obtain direct control over the political and economic activities of their new homeland, including projects to increase the religious influence of the Church of England over the North American colonies as well as plans to send garrisons to the American territories. In 1686, in order to exert a larger influence over the territories of North America, English monarch James II ordered the unification of the four New England colonies

(Massachusetts, Connecticut, Rhode Island and New Hampshire) into a Dominion of New England. The Dominion, however, was quite short-lived, as when James II was replaced as King of England by William of Orange during the Glorious Revolution of 1688, the New Englanders rebelled against their pro-King James governor and arrested him. These events, known as the Boston Revolt of 1689, were an early indication of the passions that would later lead to the American Revolution. Thereafter, it became clear in London that the colonies of New England had no intention of accepting any strict control exerted by the motherland. In the other colonial territories of North America, however, the settlers had a different opinion of Britain. In Virginia, Maryland and the Carolinas, the first colonial communities had not been created by religious dissenters, as had been the case in New England, but by settlers who were loyal to the crown and who contained a high percentage of Catholics. As a result, especially in Virginia, which had been the first royal colony of North America, British political control was much closer than in the New England colonies. In 1676, however, things also started to change in Virginia with the popular revolt commonly known as Bacon's Rebellion. This saw a clash between the Virginia militia and the royal governor of the colony, only ending after several massacres and the arrival of an English regular regiment that was tasked with restoring order. The Virginian colonists had also started to develop some sense of national identity and no longer considered themselves as part of the motherland. Consequently, 1676 can be considered a real turning point in American history: in New England, it saw the victory of the northern colonies against the natives during King Philip's War (achieved without receiving significant help from the motherland), while in Virginia, it saw the first major American rebellion against England. All this happened exactly a century before the outbreak of the American Revolution.

During the seventeenth century, while the English colonies flourished on the Atlantic coast, the French settled in Canada (at that time known as New France) and established themselves very firmly on North American soil. Differently from the English settlers, who were in search of new lands on which to expand their agricultural activities, the French settlers of Canada were more interested in obtaining control over the local fur trade. At that time, there was an increasing demand in Europe for the excellent furs obtained from the woodlands of North America, meaning fur commerce was an extremely lucrative activity. In order to obtain the best furs from the natives, the French established peaceful relations with them, which they were able to do quite easily because they did not deprive the native communities of their lands as the English colonists did further south. As a result, New France soon started to flourish commercially, and despite having a small population, it was quite strong militarily thanks to the treaties that were signed with the various native tribes living in Canada. By the end of seventeenth century, New France was ready to expand south and to menace the territorial integrity of northern New England. To face this new threat, the English colonists had no choice but to improve their militia systems and accept a larger royal military presence on their territories. Between 1689 and 1748, the English-speaking colonies of North America fought three major conflicts against the French and their numerous native allies: King William's War (1689–1697), Queen Anne's War (1702–1713) and King George's War (1740–1748). The names of these conflicts derived from the monarchs who ruled Britain when they broke out, and all were nothing other than the North American theatre of three major wars that ravaged Europe: the War of the Grand Alliance, War of the Spanish Succession and War of the Austrian Succession. They all ended without any significant changes in the political and military balance of power in North America, since the English-speaking colonies were never able to achieve a definitive victory over the French forces stationed in Canada. The key moment in the long struggle between Britain and France for control of North America came in 1754, when the French-Indian War broke out as part of the larger Seven Years' War that was fought in Europe. By that time the British colonial territories of North America had consolidated their political structures and were organized into thirteen independent entities, commonly known as the Thirteen Colonies. Until 1754, the British military presence in North America was very scarce, only two of the colonies having a royal garrison:

- New York: four independent companies of infantry, raised in 1694 and disbanded in 1763.
- South Carolina: one independent company of infantry, made up of veteran soldiers, existed from 1721–1736 in order to protect the colony from the incursions of Spanish troops garrisoning Florida. Four independent companies of infantry were sent to Charlestown during the years of King George's War.

This state of affairs came to an end in 1754, when significant British regular forces started to be sent to North America in order to fight in the French-Indian War. It is interesting to note, however, that the British Army had already recruited some regiments in the Thirteen Colonies before 1754:

Oglethorpe's Regiment of Foot: raised in Georgia during 1737 and disbanded in 1747.

Gooch's Regiment of Foot: raised from all the American colonies in 1740 and having a large establishment with four battalions. It was disbanded in 1742.

Officer of the 2nd Connecticut Provincial Regiment. (*Colour plate by Herbert Knotel, part of the Anne S.K. Brown Military Collection*)

Shirley's Regiment of Foot: raised in New England during 1745 to garrison the fortress of Louisbourg, captured from the French during King George's War. It was disbanded in 1749.

Pepperell's Regiment of Foot: raised in New England during 1745 to garrison the fortress of Louisbourg. It too was disbanded in 1749.

Naturally, each of the Thirteen Colonies was defended by its own militia units, which were much more numerous than the few British regulars deployed in North America. The militia of each colony had its own peculiar history and organization, which was influenced by the strategic position of its home territory and the main features of the colony's internal politics. The militias of some colonies, like those of Virginia and Massachusetts, had already become considerable institutions during the seventeenth century, whereas those of some of the 'younger' colonies were still small by the outbreak of the American Revolution in 1775.

Virginia: since the founding of Jamestown in 1607, it was clear to the Virginian colonists that if they wanted to survive in the New World they had to organize themselves in some sort of military structure. In 1610, the Virginia militia received its first regular establishment, being organized into six companies – or bands – of fifty men, each commanded by a captain. In addition, there was also a small Guard of Halberdiers escorting the royal governor. A training programme was set up, under which all able-bodied colonists had to train and exercise regularly with perfect military discipline. Each of the six companies in turn was on watch, fully armed and equipped, while the others performed the daily activities required for the existence of the settlement. From 1622, the militia of Virginia was completely reorganized and started to be influenced by the system of the contemporary English trained bands, albeit with some significant differences. In England, several householders could be grouped together into a single administrative unit and provide a single militiaman; in Virginia, instead, all settlers had to be armed. This practice, however, caused serious problems to the economic life of the colony, as in the event of war there would have been a chronic lack of workers in the fields. As a result, the following solution was adopted: each colonist who went on active service could rest assured that the other members of his community, who remained at home, would carry out the labours that were normally performed by him. Differently from what happened in England, where militiamen stored their weapons in local armouries or in parish churches, in Virginia they kept their arms at home. In 1629, a further refinement was added to this general organization, with the division of Virginia into four military districts (each having a local commander). Militia forces from the different districts could operate together for combined operations, but also as separate corps in order to respond to local threats. From 1651, the militia companies were assembled into county regiments; some years later, the territory of Virginia was divided into four provinces and nineteen counties. Each of the latter was to provide one regiment of infantry and one troop of horse. In addition to the militia forces, the royal governor also had a small personal guard that was commanded by a commissioned Captain of the Guard. During Bacon's Rebellion, most of the militia supported the popular rising against the autocratic Governor William Berkeley. To crush the revolt as swiftly as possible, Charles II sent to the colony an English regular unit known as Jeffery's Regiment of Foot. When this unit returned to England, two independent companies of English regulars were formed to remain in Virginia. These, however, were soon disbanded in May 1682. During this period, the first small parties of rangers started to be organized within the militia of Virginia. These, numbering around thirty men each, garrisoned the frontier forts and were mounted in order to travel long distances. They were paid in tobacco and had to provide their own arms, clothing, equipment, saddlery and horses. The general militia, meanwhile, retained its county organization for several decades. At the outbreak of the French-Indian War, the militia of Virginia comprised an impressive total of 30,000 men, but most of these were not trained and were ill-equipped. From July 1755, in order to defend the frontier areas of the colony from enemy raids, the local communities formed units of volunteers to patrol the most exposed locations. These included several companies of infantry as well as two troops of light horse/mounted infantry. An additional cavalry unit, made up of 200 volunteer gentlemen, was also raised during the course of the conflict. The members of all these corps were commonly known as 'associators', as they were private associations formed on a voluntary basis, not militia units.

Massachusetts: the settlement of Massachusetts, established in 1628, was initially relatively unopposed by the natives. From the outset, however, all able-bodied men of the new colony bore arms and were assembled into four companies. As the settlement expanded, new militia companies were organized, and in order to give some proper training to these, two military instructors were recruited in 1630. During the period October–December 1636, the militia companies of Massachusetts Bay Colony were re-ordered and formed into three regiments: the East, North and South Regiments. The East Regiment was the most important one, including militia companies from Boston and several other important centres. Despite this new organization, several independent bands continued to exist in the outlying communities of the colony. With the general growth in the number of militia units, there was a new need for specialized training. As a result, during 1637, there were proposals to set up in Boston a special unit that could provide training courses for militia officers and artillery services. The basic idea was to create something similar to the City of London's Artillery Garden, which later became known as the Honourable Artillery Company. On 13 March 1638, the colonial authorities granted a charter for the creation of the Military Company of Massachusetts, whose first commander was the veteran Captain Robert Keayne (who had served in the London Company). Under Keayne's guidance, the new company became the first military training unit/artillery school of the American colonies. In 1643, the general organization of the militia was changed again with the creation of new county regiments that bore the names of their respective counties. As in the rest of the North American colonies, cavalry appeared in Massachusetts only at a later date: this happened around 1650, when horses started to become increasingly common in New England and a first troop of horse was formed (whose members were ordinary militiamen who acted as mounted soldiers only when their own county regiment was not on exercise). During the following years, more troops of horses were formed: by 1667 there were twelve, with 160 cavalrymen each. The area of present-day Maine remained part of Massachusetts until 1820, its militia, which was composed by around 700 men in 1670, being organized into independent companies that were formally part of the Massachusetts militia. By 1676, the latter's strength was estimated at 40,000 able-bodied men, aged 16–60. These trained eight times each year, while the artillerymen that each major town possessed trained every week. In the following decades, as a result of the emergency faced during King Philip's War, the Massachusetts militia continued to expand as the colony grew and more county regiments were formed. In 1744, a total of 150 militiamen from the various county regiments were chosen in order to form an independent company of grenadiers, which was attached to the York County Regiment. By the mid-eighteenth century, the Military Company of Massachusetts had transformed itself into an independent militia company made up of Boston's most prominent merchants, and had gradually lost its original functions. Meanwhile, a new Train of Artillery comprising volunteer gunners had been created to serve the guns of Boston. This unit was attached to the Boston Militia Regiment, together with an independent company of grenadiers. In 1728, a ceremonial military corps, known as the Boston Cadet Company, had also been formed to provide the escort for the governor of the colony, being made up of young gentlemen. A similar unit of cadets was later organized in the city of Great Barrington. During 1754, the personal guard of the Massachusetts governor was expanded with the formation of a Company of Horse Guards, made up of young gentlemen from Boston.

Private of the Massachusetts Provincial Regiment. (*Colour plate by Herbert Knotel, part of the Anne S.K. Brown Military Collection*)

New Hampshire: the first settlements established in New Hampshire dated back to 1623. From the beginning, the settlers of this colony had to face serious military threats from the natives and pirates who were active in the region. In 1631, a professional soldier was invited to the new settlements in order to organize the local militia and train the colonists. Ten years later, however, New Hampshire passed under the jurisdiction of Massachusetts and lost its autonomy. It became again independent only in 1679, when it was separated from Massachusetts by royal order. As a consequence, on 16 March 1680, the independent militia of New Hampshire was re-formed, initially consisting of one foot company for each of the four major settlements (Portsmouth, Dover, Exeter and Hampton), plus an artillery company and a troop of horse stationed in Portsmouth. The cavalry troop, however, was disbanded a few years later. With the growth of the colony, more militia companies were formed, these all being grouped together in the New Hampshire Regiment of Militia in 1689. By 1730, the militia of New Hampshire was made up of two infantry regiments, which were supplemented during the following decades by some small independent detachments of scouts that were created to patrol the frontier areas. In 1748, these had a total of 174 men. A troop of horse was raised from the inhabitants of Kingston in 1750 and was added to the existing militia units. With the outbreak of the French-Indian War, the New Hampshire militia was greatly expanded and came to comprise nine regiments of infantry as well as one regiment of cavalry.

Connecticut: led by Thomas Hooker, some 250 colonists from Massachusetts settled on the west bank of the Connecticut River in early 1636. One of the reasons why Hooker had left Massachusetts Bay Colony was that only members of the Puritan Church could vote and participate in the government of the colony; he believed, instead, that any adult male owning property should have had the right to vote and take part in the political life of his community. No militia was initially formed by the Connecticut colonists, but relations with the local natives soon became increasingly difficult. As a result, the settlers were ordered to assemble for training once a month and were organized into companies. By 1650, these companies included more or less 800 men, and they were supplemented by a troop of horse raised in Hartford during 1658. Following the short-lived Dutch capture of New York in 1673, Connecticut's colonial authorities ordered that 500 militiamen (more or less a third of the colony's militia at that time) had to be mounted to patrol the coast. During King Philip's War, Connecticut contributed to the war efforts of New England by sending a force of 315 militiamen. In addition, some 350 militia dragoons (mounted infantrymen) were employed against the natives; these men had to provide horses, weapons, equipment and clothes for themselves, but could be compensated by the colonial authorities in case of the loss of their properties. During the central years of Queen Anne's War, 800 Connecticut militiamen patrolled the frontier of their colony (on horseback during summer, on snowshoes during winter). In 1739, the Connecticut militia was reorganized into thirteen infantry regiments, formed by assembling the companies raised in the various settlements. Each of these regiments was to have an attached troop of horse. During this same period, the students of Yale College organized an artillery company that was known as the College Artillery. Some years later, another independent artillery company was established in New London.

Rhode Island: in January 1636, Salem minister Roger Williams was banished from Massachusetts because of his theological differences with the ruling class of the colony. He had preached that government and religion should be separated and believed that the natives had been treated by the English settlers with no justice. After being exiled from Massachusetts, Williams bought some land for establishing a new colony in present-day Providence, Rhode Island. Williams and his group of colonists settled at the tip of Narragansett Bay, the new site being called Providence Plantation (which soon became a place of religious freedom). From the early days of the Providence settlement, the Rhode Island colonists gave great importance to their military organization but had very few opportunities to gain combat experience. Some volunteer units of cavalry and artillery – including the Island Troop of Horse, formed in 1667 at Newport and disbanded a few years later – were gradually added to the original infantry companies: the Providence Troop of Horse (1719), the King's County Troop of Horse (1730), the Artillery Company of Newport (1741), the Artillery Company of Providence (1744), the 1st Newport Troop of Horse (1746), the Westerly/Charlestown Artillery Company (1755), the Newport Infantry Company (1755) and the 2nd Newport Troop of Horse (1760).

Maryland: the colony of Maryland was founded in 1634 by a group of English Catholic refugees, under a charter obtained from King Charles I. By 1638, the St Mary Colony had its own trained band of militiamen numbering 120 men. During the following years, the militia was expanded and received a better organization: in the early 1640s, for example, captains were appointed for every 100 men. In April 1650, the Maryland legislative assembly ordered the establishment of a small full-time garrison of six men (under a captain) in the strategic fort located at St Inigo Harbour. In March 1655, Maryland saw the beginning of a strong internal clash between Puritan and Catholic settlers, which ended with victory for the Puritans at the Battle of the Severn River. After the end of hostilities, the militia was ordered to disarm any inhabitant suspected of disaffection towards the colony's new Puritan government.

Grenadier officer (left) and musketeer (right) of the New Jersey Provincial Regiment. (*Colour plate by Herbert Knotel, part of the Anne S.K. Brown Military Collection*)

As a result, Catholics, Quakers and Baptists were disarmed and their rights of citizenship were denied. On 12 July 1658, the independent militia companies of Maryland were assembled into two regiments, known as the Northern Regiment and the Southern Regiment. There also was an independent Governor's Own Company, which performed guard duties. With the progressive expansion of the colony, new county regiments of militia were established, which included troops of cavalry and dragoons in addition to the usual foot companies. From 1692, a number of rangers started to be posted to the forts built along the frontier with the native territories. With the outbreak of the French-Indian War, the militia of Maryland was expanded with the formation of some volunteer units tasked with patrolling the frontier. These corps, however, were all quite short-lived.

New York: this colony, which had previously been known as New Netherlands because it had been created by the Dutch, came under definitive English control only in 1674. The Militia Act of 1677 prescribed the raising of 6,000 militiamen organized into several independent companies, 2,000 of whom were to be mounted. However, this high number of horse militiamen soon became impossible to sustain from an economic point of view and was rapidly reduced. In November 1700, the militia of New York mustered a total of 3,182 men, organized into eight county regiments: City and County of New York, City and County of Albany, Suffolk, Queen's, King's, Richmond, West Chester and the combined counties of Ulster and Duchess. In addition to these foot regiments, there were mounted units in New York, Albany, Queen's, King's, Ulster and Duchess Counties. During the period 1700–1770, the militia of New York was gradually expanded with the formation of several new units. Shortly before the outbreak of the American Revolution, it comprised the following formations: twenty-six regiments of infantry, eleven troops of cavalry and some independent companies of artillery (for a total of 32,000 men). The best of the few artillery companies was that stationed in New York, also known as Blue Company from the colour of its uniform. Some units made up of volunteers also existed, plus one independent company of grenadiers in New York (The New York City Grenadiers) and a similar one in Albany.

New Jersey: this colony became predominantly inhabited by English settlers only in 1664. Being under no serious military threat and having a very small population, it developed its militia units quite slowly. A Militia Act passed in 1730 improved the general organization of the few existing companies, but they were never assembled into larger units until the outbreak of the American Revolution.

Pennsylvania: the first English settlers arrived in Pennsylvania during the late 1660s and organized a small militia of some sort in 1669. The few able-bodied men of the early settlements later came under the New York militia law in 1676, thus having no independent militia structure. The real colonization of Pennsylvania, however, started only in 1681 when the territory was chartered to William Penn of the Society of Friends (a religious group commonly known in England as the Quakers). These were all pacifists, who believed that no man could kill another for any reason. Being persecuted

Officer (left) and musketeer (right) of the New York Provincial Regiment. (*Colour plate by Herbert Knotel, part of the Anne S.K. Brown Military Collection*)

in England for their religious beliefs, they followed the example of the Puritans and obtained the charter for a territory in North America. The Commonwealth of Pennsylvania was unique among the English colonies of North America, having no military forces and no militia laws. A few of Pennsylvania's settlers were not Quakers and thus bore arms for personal defence, but they were a small minority. Attempts to raise volunteers from the colony during Queen Anne's War failed completely, and the first militia units of Pennsylvania were raised only in 1744. These were quite different from those of the other colonies, since they consisted of volunteers who were paid by the colonial government for their weapons and other expenses. These volunteers were assembled into small companies with fifty or 100 men each. In 1747, a young Benjamin Franklin contributed to the raising of such volunteer units, organizing a corps of 600 men assembled into eleven infantry companies. This was known as the Associated Regiment of Philadelphia and its members were called The Associators. A similar regiment, with nine infantry companies, was soon after raised from the countryside of Philadelphia. Benjamin Franklin's example was later followed in all the counties of Pennsylvania, and the following associated corps were organized: one regiment with thirty-three companies in Lancaster County, one regiment with twenty-six companies in Chester County and one regiment with eighteen companies in Buck's County. The Associated Regiment of Philadelphia also included two companies of artillery, which were tasked with manning the two batteries that protected the city. With the end of King George's War, however, the Associated corps were all disbanded and the interesting military experiment organized by Benjamin Franklin came to an end. In 1755, the first Militia Law of Pennsylvania was approved, but this did not change the existing situation in any significant way since service in the militia remained voluntary. During 1756, one infantry company and one artillery company, having a permanent character, were raised for service in Philadelphia. These were later supplemented by another company of infantry and a single troop of cavalry. The new Militia Law passed in 1757 made military service in the militia compulsory for Pennsylvania, but this was never put in practice. As a result, to defend at least the frontier settlements from native raiders, one volunteer company of rangers had to be established during 1763. A unit of volunteer frontiersmen, known as Paxton Boys, was also formed in that year to fight against the natives. This unit had a semi-regular status and massacred many natives without good reason: as a result, they were soon disbanded after threatening to march on the city of Philadelphia. To face the Paxton Boys, Benjamin Franklin re-formed the Associated Regiment of Philadelphia, which now had 1,000 volunteers in six companies of infantry, two companies of cavalry and one company of artillery. After these events, the Associated Regiment was again disbanded, being re-established only in 1775 with the outbreak of the American Revolution.

Delaware: originally settled by Swedes, Delaware became part of the New Netherlands Colony like the rest of New Sweden. Following the English conquest of 1664, Delaware became part of New York Colony. During this period, the colonial settlements of Delaware were quite small and had very few inhabitants. From 1669, some militia companies were established as part of New York's larger militia, but Delaware was separated from New York in 1682 and absorbed into Pennsylvania. William Penn allowed the area to have its own legislative assembly, which soon made Delaware an autonomous colony. Having different religious beliefs from the Quakers of Pennsylvania, the settlers of Delaware continued to have their own independent companies of militia. These companies remained very few until 1775, since the population of the colony was quite small.

Musketeer of the North Carolina Provincial Regiment. (*Colour plate by Herbert Knotel, part of the Anne S.K. Brown Military Collection*)

North Carolina: the territories of the future colonies of North Carolina, South Carolina and Georgia were granted as a single Carolina Colony in 1629. English expansion over these southern areas was not very rapid, with real colonization taking place only during the 1670s. According to the 1669 Constitution of Carolina, all able-bodied men aged 17–60 had to bear arms and serve in the militia when necessary. Two militia companies were soon formed, which gradually expanded over the years due to the menace represented by the local natives. In 1673, a cavalry unit known as the Governor's Horse Guard was formed. By 1685, the military of Carolina included two militia regiments (named Northward and Southward) and the Governor's Horse Guard. Later, an independent militia company was added, comprising Huguenots (French Protestants) who had fled from France because of the religious persecution organized against them by Louis XIV. According to the 1696 Militia Act, companies were to drill at least every two months and regiments were to assemble once a year. When the Spanish and French attacked Charleston in 1706, during Queen Anne's War, the local militia of what would later become South Carolina included 1,500 men: two companies from Charleston, seven from the Northward Regiment and one from the Southward Regiment. In 1704, the Patrol Act ordered that ten men from each militia company had to serve on horse, in order to patrol their districts and prevent enemy raids or slave uprisings. In 1710, Carolina's territory was divided into North Carolina and South Carolina; in the former, which was sparsely inhabited, the first militia law was passed only in 1715. Despite this, the militia of North Carolina was not mobilized until 1754. During the French-Indian War, however, it could muster just a few men with superficial training and outdated equipment. From 1764, some small corps of rangers were formed to patrol the frontier areas of the colony, but the general situation of the militia did not change until the outbreak of the American Revolution.

South Carolina: in 1710, the organization of this colony's militia was still the same of 1706, with 1,500 men, as the elite Governor's Horse Guard became part of South Carolina's military units. In 1716, these were supplemented by two independent companies of mounted rangers, which were tasked with patrolling the western frontier of the colony. From 1719, trusted black slaves were authorized to serve in the militia, which was unique in the military history of the Thirteen Colonies. Acts of bravery from the black militiamen could be rewarded with the granting of freedom to the individual who had distinguished himself in combat. In 1740, however, this social experiment came to an end after the putting down of a major slave revolt. During 1739, a second troop of the Governor's Horse Guard had been raised, followed by a third in 1740 and a fourth in 1743. At the beginning of King George's War, the militia of South Carolina comprised five infantry regiments, which were later augmented to seven (having a total of ninety-two companies). By 1774, another five regiments had been added to this general establishment. In 1760, seven independent companies (with seventy-five mounted rangers each) were raised from volunteer militiamen, but these were all disbanded by 1762. During 1765 and 1766, the Charleston Regiment had two additional companies, one of grenadiers and one of light infantry; both were disbanded quite soon, but the light infantry company was re-formed in 1773. The Governor's Horse Guard assumed the new denomination of the Regiment of Horse Militia in 1750 and was reduced to just three troops. In 1756, some gentlemen from Charleston organized a volunteer artillery company; finally, during 1761, a small constabulary corps known as the Watch Company was also formed in order to keep order in Charleston.

Georgia: this colony was created in 1733 as a buffer zone between Spanish Florida and South Carolina. Its militia started to be properly organized only after the end of King George's War, when four independent companies of volunteers were raised in Savannah (three of infantry and one of artillery). A single company of rangers, patrolling the frontier, existed from 1734. In 1739, due to the outbreak of hostilities with Spain, another two units of rangers were formed: the Troop of English Rangers and the Troop of Highland Rangers. These were later supplemented by a Highland Independent Company of Foot (which became the nucleus of the Georgia Rangers, analyzed in a previous chapter). As is clear from their name, the two Highland corps were recruited from Scottish settlers. In 1740, the Marine Company of Boatmen was created to patrol the inland waterways of Georgia. During the French-Indian War, the ordinary infantry companies were increased to eight, but after the end of hostilities the militia of Georgia remained very small until the outbreak of the American Revolution.

When the French-Indian War began, the authorities of the Thirteen Colonies were forced to recruit large numbers of new military units in addition to their ordinary militia. This conflict was fought on a large scale and most of its operations took place in remote areas of North America. The militia units were organized and trained to fight only for short periods and not far from their home territory, so a new category of American fighting force had to be created. These were the Provincial Troops, or simply Provincials, permanent full-time units that were available for conducting extended operations far from their home colony. Most of the new Provincial units were recruited through a quota system that was applied to the existing militia. Generally, they were made up of the best militiamen who were interested in having a military career. The Provincials had a lot in common with the regular regiments of

Musketeer of the Pennsylvania Provincial Regiment. (*Colour plate by Herbert Knotel, part of the Anne S.K. Brown Military Collection*)

the British Army, but were temporary formations that were usually disbanded when the campaign or war for which they had been mobilized came to an end. In this sense, they were similar to the original militia units. Some early Provincial Troops had already been organized during the 1745 expedition against the French fortress of Louisbourg, when the following units were formed:

- Massachusetts: seven infantry regiments;
- New Hampshire: one infantry regiment;
- Connecticut: one infantry regiment;
- Rhode Island: three infantry companies.

Following the capture of Louisbourg, the American colonies decided to assemble a larger military force to attempt an invasion of Canada. The campaign ended in failure, but led to the formation of the following units:

- Massachusetts: two infantry regiments with twenty-seven companies;
- Connecticut: one infantry regiment with ten companies;
- New Hampshire: one infantry regiment with nine companies;
- Rhode Island: three independent infantry companies;
- New York: thirty-one independent infantry companies;
- New Jersey: five independent infantry companies;
- Maryland: three independent infantry companies;
- Pennsylvania: four independent infantry companies;
- Virginia: one independent infantry company.

The number of Provincials raised during the French-Indian War was much more impressive, each of the Thirteen Colonies contributing to the war effort as follows:

Connecticut: the first two infantry regiments were raised in 1755, followed by another two later the same year. In 1757, another temporary infantry regiment was added, but this was disbanded in 1758. The original four units were maintained until 1761, when they were reduced to two regiments supplemented by two independent infantry companies. All corps were disbanded in 1763.

Delaware: 300 Provincials were raised for the campaign of 1758.

Georgia: this colony provided only two companies of rangers and one troop of cavalry, due to its limited population.

Maryland: in 1754, a single company of rangers was mobilized, followed by 200 Provincials to carry out garrison duties. An infantry battalion was established in 1755.

Massachusetts: initially, this colony raised a single infantry regiment containing two independent battalions. During 1755, another two infantry regiments with 500 men each were organized, together with a small artillery train consisting of the following elements: one captain, one lieutenant, one assistant, three NCOs and sixteen gunners. For the campaign of 1756, the Provincials of Massachusetts were greatly expanded, being reorganized as seven infantry regiments with 500 soldiers each and two artillery companies with 110 men each. In 1757, the infantry was reduced to a single regiment, having a large establishment with 1,800 soldiers in seventeen. Massachusetts' war effort reached its peak in 1758 with the raising of seven infantry regiments of 1,000 men each. In 1759, the Provincial infantry of the colony was reorganized on eight regiments and four independent companies. These were supplemented by 300 pioneers having auxiliary duties. During 1760 the infantry regiments were reduced to five, and then to three in 1761. In addition, a small independent infantry company was garrisoned in Boston from 1757.

New Hampshire: initially, the Provincials of New Hampshire consisted of two infantry regiments, one independent infantry company with garrison duties and one company of rangers. In 1756, the foot regiments were reduced to just one and the ranger company was re-formed. One battalion and an independent company of infantry were added to the existing units in 1757, both having garrison duties. A single company of carpenters and three companies of rangers were also raised. From 1758–1760, New Hampshire continued to provide a single infantry regiment.

New Jersey: at the beginning of hostilities, the colony raised a single battalion of infantry and a Frontier Guard made up of 400 soldiers. During 1756, the infantry unit was expanded and became a regiment, then a new company of rangers was formed in the following year. Before the end of hostilities in 1762, New Jersey also contributed with the creation of an independent infantry company that had garrison duties.

New York: in 1755, a single regiment of infantry was organized, which was re-raised for the campaigns of 1756 and 1757. During 1758, the establishment of this single unit was expanded to three battalions. The original New York Regiment was reduced to two battalions in 1759, but the following year another three short-lived infantry regiments were formed.

North Carolina: at the outbreak of the French-Indian War, the colony raised a single (weak) regiment of infantry. This was soon supplemented by a ranger company and a small garrison company (tasked with frontier defence). Another three independent infantry companies were formed later, and were merged with the existing one in order to establish a battalion. In 1757, the Provincials of North Carolina were reduced to just two independent companies with fifty men each; during the following year, however, a new infantry battalion was raised (which continued to be supported by two garrison companies). In 1759, only the latter remained active, each having just thirty men. During 1761, an infantry regiment with seven companies was raised, but this was quite short-lived.

Pennsylvania: in 1754, this colony had no proper militia to speak of, since it had always been dominated by pacifist Quakers. An organization of volunteers, created by Benjamin Franklin and known as the Associated Companies, provided military services to the colony's government. Very soon, however, three Provincial infantry battalions were raised in Pennsylvania in order to fight against the French. In 1757, these were reduced to two and were grouped into a single regiment. A third battalion was re-formed in 1758, and the internal establishment of all battalions was expanded (the first had twelve companies, the second thirteen and the third seventeen). The first two battalions also had an attached troop of cavalry.

Rhode Island: this colony initially contributed a single infantry regiment, which was re-raised in 1756. During the same year a second infantry regiment, with 400 soldiers, was also organized. In 1757, the establishment of two infantry regiments was confirmed and one company of rangers was also added. In addition, one reserve battalion with 250 men was organized (to be used only in case of need). Between 1758 and 1760, Rhode Island contributed to the British war effort with a single infantry regiment, which maintained a standard establishment of 1,000 soldiers.

South Carolina: the first Provincials of this territory were raised only in 1760, when seven troops of mounted rangers were formed to fight against the natives along the frontier. Soon afterwards, a small infantry regiment was organized, which continued to serve until 1761.

Virginia: in 1754, the colony raised its first Provincial military unit, the famous Virginia Regiment, which was later commanded by Colonel George Washington. This soon proved to be an excellent unit and participated in the Braddock's Expedition of 1755. During this campaign, however, the Virginia Regiment (with

Musketeer of the Virginia Provincial Regiment. (*Colour plate by Herbert Knotel, part of the Anne S.K. Brown Military Collection*)

ten companies) was defeated and suffered severe losses at the Battle of Monogahela. Virginia also contributed to military operations in the Ohio River Valley with six companies of foot rangers, one company of mounted rangers and two companies of carpenters. The Virginia Regiment was rapidly re-raised, this time with an expanded establishment of sixteen companies. In 1758, the 2nd Virginia Regiment was formed, the original one remaining under the command of Colonel Washington. The new regiment was disbanded in 1759 and a reserve force of 500 soldiers was established. Before the end of the French-Indian War, three independent companies of frontier guards were also raised.

During the eighteenth century, the Thirteen Colonies were not the only British colonial possessions in the Americas, which also included some of the Caribbean islands collectively known as the West Indies. Economically, this was one of the most profitable areas in the world. Having been colonized by the European powers for many decades, they produced large amounts of sugar, which was sold around the globe at very high prices. Additionally, albeit on a smaller scale, they produced other very profitable crops such as indigo and coffee. Several of these islands were colonies of Great Britain, representing about one-third of the country's foreign trade. Thanks to the direct taxes and duties from the Caribbean colonies, Britain was able to become the most important of the colonial powers during the eighteenth century, and it was absolutely vital for the crown to protect such a lucrative portion of the ever-expanding British Empire. This became particularly true when, following the outbreak of the Grand Alliance War, the British West Indies started to be menaced by the French and the Spaniards, who had their own flourishing colonies in the Caribbean. Operating in the West Indies, however, was not an easy undertaking for the British Army: the local tropical climate was unsustainable for European troops, who were frequently decimated by terrible local diseases such as tropical fevers. As a result, British soldiers preferred avoiding service in the West Indies due to the unhealthy local living conditions. To solve this problem and to garrison the crown's possessions in that part of the world, the British Army had no choice but to raise military units from the local communities of free blacks, who were accustomed to the climate and temperatures of the Caribbean and thus could easily live in that theatre of operations. It was only in 1793, however, that the British raised their first military units of free blacks in the West Indies; until then, the islands were garrisoned by independent infantry companies made up of white regulars. The independent colonial companies serving in the West Indies, differently from the few that were deployed in North America, were not recruited from colonists but from British individuals who usually lived on the margins of society. Furthermore, the officers of the independent colonial companies were not particularly brilliant, since they usually only offered to raise such units to receive a commission in the regular army without having to spend money to purchase it (as was common practice in the rest of the British Army). On paper, the independent colonial companies had the same internal organization as the standard line infantry units, but in practice they usually had incomplete establishments. Between 1717 and 1720, after having been sporadically garrisoned by small detachments sent from Europe or by short-lived independent companies, the island colonies of the British West Indies finally received small but permanent garrisons. These consisted of four independent colonial companies, distributed as follows: two in Jamaica, one in the Bahamas and one in the Bermudas. From 1735–1743, the number of companies stationed in Jamaica was increased to eight, mostly because the authorities on the island feared the outbreak of a major slave uprising. By the beginning of the Seven Years' War, the following independent colonial companies were stationed in the British West Indies: five in Jamaica, one in the Bahamas and one in the Bermudas. Later in the conflict, the British occupied the French colony of Guadeloupe in the West Indies, as well as that of Senegal in West Africa, both of which were quickly garrisoned by four independent colonial companies.

Chapter 12

The Troops of the East India Company

The British presence in India only became a significant one from the mid-eighteenth century, particularly after the Battle of Plassey in 1757. Until then, other European colonial powers such as France and Portugal had been exerting a greater influence over India than Great Britain. Since the times of the first territorial acquisitions in the Indian subcontinent, the British government had not annexed any Indian territory as a direct possession of the crown, the British territories in India all being under the control of the East India Company. Established in 1600, the East India Company was a joint-stock company that originally had as its main objective that of trading with the rich countries of the Asian continent. Like its Dutch equivalent operating in present-day Indonesia, the British East India Company gradually emerged as a regional power in Asia and expanded its commercial influence by using political and military measures. As time progressed, the British traders started to occupy some important cities in India as well as some tracts of coastline. All these new territories acted as outposts for the economic activities of the company and were also the centres from which the British could exert their influence over the local Indian rulers. By the mid-eighteenth century, with the decline of the great Moghul Empire, India was splintered into a multitude of independent princedoms. These states had outdated armies using traditional Indian weaponry and tactics, which were no match for the modern military technologies employed by the British. In consequence, the East India Company could gradually use its great resources to transform several of the Indian native states into protectorates. Thanks to the signing of favourable treaties concerning trade, the British acquired direct control over an increasing number of cities and territories. Following the great victory at Plassey, after which the French were expelled from most of India, the British expanded their possessions towards the interior areas of the subcontinent. As a result of this, during the following decades, the East India Company was forced to reorganize its military forces, which had initially been very small with a main task of protecting the commercial interests of the company and garrisoning its territorial possessions. Since their foundation, the military forces of the company included a large number of native soldiers, recruited with the help of the local rulers who were allies of the company and making up a private military organization that was not part of the British Army. On many occasions, the European and native components of the East India Company's forces cooperated very well together and showed admirable efficiency on the field of battle. With the reorganization that followed Plassey, they also started to have significant numbers and their standards of service became comparable to those of contemporary European armies. The units at the service of the company could be European ones, largely made up of soldiers from Britain, or native corps recruited from the local population but having British officers. The Indian soldiers serving European powers, be they Hindus or Muslims, were commonly known as sepoys. Generally speaking, the European soldiers recruited by the company in Britain were not of the same quality as those who served in the regular British Army, which offered better conditions of service to recruits and thus attracted to the ranks the best elements wishing to serve in the military. Most of the British soldiers serving under the flags of the company were individuals who had decided to leave their home country in search of an opportunity and who lived at the margins of society. Some of them had experienced problems with justice while others had no choice but to enlist as soldiers of fortune in order to earn a living. The members of the European military units, however, also included significant numbers of whites who were recruited from the many European adventurers or mercenaries who were in search of employment in India. French, Swiss, German and Dutch recruits were the most commonly found, but there were also individuals of mixed ancestry (half European and half Indian). Discipline and training of these soldiers were not exactly the same as their equivalents serving in the British Army, but on most occasions these men proved to be reliable fighters. A good number of them had a clear idea of what military discipline was, since it was not uncommon for a soldier from the regular army to join the company's forces after his period of service in the British Army had ended. Life in India was cheaper than in Britain and the risks faced while serving under the flags of the company were not comparable to those experienced in the regular army.

From the early eighteenth century, the territorial possessions of the British East India Company were organized into three autonomous presidencies: Madras, Bengal and Bombay. Each of these had its own army, comprising several military units. In 1721, Madras had three European infantry companies, which included a substantial number of Eurasians, but there was also a small artillery corps comprising a number of native lascars or workers. In 1748, the forces of Madras were expanded with the addition of two new infantry companies recruited from Swiss professional soldiers and reorganized as a single battalion of infantry and one company of artillery. In 1758, the infantry was expanded with the addition of another two battalions, then the three existing foot units were restructured in 1774 as two infantry regiments with

European infantryman of the East India Company. (*Anne S.K. Brown Military Collection*)

two battalions each. The artillery was expanded to two companies in 1752 and then to three in 1765. At the beginning of the Seven Years' War, the European infantry of Bengal consisted of a single company with 150 men, most of whom were Dutch or Eurasians, while the artillery comprised a single company that was completely destroyed in 1756 but was soon re-raised. As a result of the above, when Robert Clive, the victor of the Battle of Plassey, assumed command of the East India Company's forces in Bengal, the situation he found was far from a positive one. After the victorious campaign of 1757, however, the European infantry of Bengal was increased to a full battalion and the artillery was expanded to two companies. In 1765, the number of artillery companies was increased to four, while in 1778 five new infantry battalions were recruited. The original European garrison of Bombay consisted of four infantry companies, which were increased to eight by 1742. The first artillery company was created in 1748. After the Seven Years' War, the existing infantry companies were consolidated into a single battalion, and by 1788 the European foot troops of Bombay consisted of two regiments. The artillery was increased to three companies in 1755. In Bombay, the European

European artillery officer of the Madras Presidency, wearing solar *topee*. (*Anne S.K. Brown Military Collection*)

Sepoy infantryman of the Madras Presidency. (*Anne S.K. Brown Military Collection*)

infantry, despite its denomination, included several soldiers of mixed descent known as 'Topasses'.

During the first half of the eighteenth century, each of the armies of the East India Company's presidencies recruited auxiliary infantry companies of Indian native soldiers when needed, most notably during times of war. These sepoy corps had a temporary and semi-regular nature. The combat experiences of the Seven Years' War and the Battle of Plassey, however, highlighted to the company's authorities the great potential of the locally recruited contingents. Consequently, from 1757, the existing independent and temporary companies of sepoys were consolidated into permanent battalions having European officers and superior discipline. In the Bengal army, most of the sepoys were Hindus of high caste, who came in great numbers from the Indian provinces bordering Bengal. In Madras and Bombay, however, the sepoys did not only come from Hindu high castes, instead including large numbers of Muslims. Generally speaking, all the native soldiers at the service of the East India Company came from the so-called martial races of India, social groups characterized by specific ethnic and cultural features, which were traditionally linked with the profession of soldiery in India. Under Clive's orders, Bengal was the first presidency to assemble its sepoy companies into a battalion soon after the Battle of Plassey. By 1762, the number of native infantry battalions in Bengal had risen to twenty-one, but this was reduced to eighteen in 1763 after three

Sepoy officer (left) and private (right) of the Bengal Presidency, wearing sundial turban. (*Anne S.K. Brown Military Collection*)

Sepoy infantryman of the Bengal Presidency, wearing bell-shaped turban. (*Anne S.K. Brown Military Collection*)

of the existing units were disbanded following a mutiny. The native infantry of Madras was grouped into two permanent battalions during 1759, each of them comprising eight companies of fusiliers and one of grenadiers. In 1759, the number of sepoy battalions in Madras was increased to six, and the expansion continued after the end of the Seven Years' War so that by 1767 there were nineteen battalions of native infantry in the presidency. Bombay was slower than the other two presidencies in establishing independent companies of sepoys, and it was only in 1768 that the first two battalions of native infantry were created. These were increased to four during the following years.

Initially, the East India Company did not raise any cavalry unit for service in its colonial possessions, since maintaining mounted units had enormous economic costs. However, it soon became apparent that large numbers of Indian auxiliaries were available for organizing into some small but efficient cavalry corps. In 1748, the first troop of cavalry was raised in Madras; this, consisting of Europeans, was disbanded in 1752 but was re-formed in 1758. In 1761, the number of troops was increased to four, each consisting of five officers and sixty other ranks. In 1772, the European cavalry of Madras was disbanded. From 1767, Madras could also count on eight cavalry regiments – each with 500 men – provided by the Nawab of Arcot (an ally of the East India Company), although these were reduced to four following a mutiny. Bengal's cavalry consisted of just three troops of native horsemen, known as the Moghul Horse since their members were equipped as heavy cavalrymen in the Moghuls' traditional style (with metal helmets and cuirasses). These three troops of native cavalry were disbanded in 1772. Bombay did not have any mounted unit. Each of the three presidencies had its own informal Engineer Corps, consisting of a small number of British officers having specific technical competences. These were in charge of a labour force consisting of lascars recruited from the local Indian communities.

Chapter 13

Uniforms and Equipment

Among the troops of the various European armies, the British soldiers of 1727–1760 probably wore the smartest and most distinctive uniforms of their age. Scarlet red, the characteristic colour of the English infantry since the years of Cromwell's New Model Army, was worn by all the foot regiments. The standard headgear of the musketeers was the black tricorn hat, which had a narrow lace on the external edge in white or yellow – silver or gold for officers – and a button made of white metal or yellow brass at the left front. The button was placed over a black cockade, which had a black loop for rankers and a golden one for officers. The headgear of the grenadiers was the mitre cap, entirely made of cloth and having a tall front mounted on shaped stiffened card; the front was embroidered with the Royal cypher surmounted by a crown and encircled by foliate decorative designs. At the bottom of the front face there was a small red flap embroidered with the motto '*Nec Aspera Terrent*' ('difficulties be damned') and with the white horse of Hanover. The main body of the mitre cap was in the distinctive facing colour of each regiment, while the various decorations were in the regiment's distinctive lace colour (white being the most common). Each unit had peculiar facing and lace colours. At the top of the headgear was a white woollen tuft with a centre of threads in the distinctive facing colour of each regiment. The rear of the cap had a piece of red cloth stitched to the stiffened front and two pieces of cane used to retain the shape of the headgear. Coloured tape was placed over the sides and back of the cap to conceal the stitching. At the rear of the headgear there was also a tape in the facing colour bearing the number of the unit, a flaming grenade and some other foliate decorative designs. The mitre cap had a strip of regimental lace running around its bottom edge. To prevent the headgear from falling off, it was usually fitted with tapes sewn into the lining which were tied under the plait of the soldier's hair. The caps of grenadier officers were decorated with silver or golden thread. The few regiments designated as fusiliers had all their companies wearing the mitre cap.

The grenadiers of the Highland infantry units wore a distinctive fur cap rather than the standard mitre cap. This black bearskin had the fur rising towards the top in a tapered point, and on the rear it carried a red patch that was often embroidered with the regimental number or a regimental symbol (usually in white). On the front, the fur cap had a red or black lacquered plate, which was ornamented with white metal decorations. The latter usually consisted of the British coat-of-arms with the letters 'G' and 'R' on the sides – for 'George Rex' – placed under the motto '*Nec Aspera Terrent*'. The pattern of the decorations, however, could vary greatly from unit to unit. The bearskin was also decorated with knotted worsted cords and tassels, which were suspended on the right side of the headgear. The cords and tassels were silver for officers, gilt for NCOs and white for rankers. On the back of the cap, under the red patch, was a metal badge, which consisted of a flaming grenade. Sometimes, a short white plume could be worn on the left side of the headgear. The musketeers of the Highland regiments did not wear the standard tricorn as headgear, instead having the distinctive Highland bonnet made of heavy blue wool. This was round and soft, having a coloured pompom ('tourie') at the centre of the crown. On the left side it usually bore a black cockade, which could be surmounted by a short plume of the same colour. Over time, a 3-inch-wide chequered band of white, red and green dicing was added around the base of each bonnet. Curiously, the naval infantry regiments raised in 1739 and 1740 had all their companies wearing mitre caps that were similar to those worn by the grenadier companies of the light regiments, but the decorative designs embroidered on their front were simpler and had alternative badges in place of the white horse of Hanover. The 60th Regiment of Foot had the standard tricorn of the line infantry units, while the new light infantry regiments and companies formed during the Seven Years' War wore distinctive caps made of black leather. These, being visored, were similar to the contemporary jockey's caps, usually having a black leather plate on the front and the back. The front plate bore the Royal cypher over the number of the regiment. The light infantry caps could have a rigid crest decorated with a coloured plume; each light infantry unit had its own distinctive model of leather cap, so there were many variations.

The standard coat worn by the British infantrymen, based on the contemporary prevailing civilian style, was quite voluminous, like those worn by the foot soldiers of other nations. It was full-skirted, having tails that extended as far as the knees. Most of the infantry regiments had coats with frontal lapels, which were designed to button across the chest in bad weather, although a few regiments had coats without lapels. The lapels were dyed in the distinctive facing colour of each regiment, which was royal blue for the three regiments of guard infantry and for all those units that bore the adjective 'Royal' in their official denomination. The colour of the foot soldiers' coats was the universal scarlet red, which was relatively costly to produce but quite elegant. The coats were collarless and had cuffs of the Swedish pattern, i.e. they were gauntlet-shaped and quite voluminous. Like the frontal lapels, the cuffs were also dyed in the distinctive facing colour of each regiment. The coloured lapels ended in a point in the upper part, which was held in position by a single button; along each lapel there were six buttons, which could be white metal or brass yellow. The six buttonholes of each lapel were decorated with lace loops, which were in the distinctive lacing colour of each regiment (white being the most common). The coat, on the front and around the neck, was piped in the lacing colour, as were the lapels. Under the lapels, each coat had another three buttons with the usual lace loops. The cuffs, V-shaped, could have one or more stripes of lace in the distinctive colour of each regiment. Above the cuff, a cuff flap having a variable number of buttons (usually three or five) was visible, with piping and lace loops of the buttonholes in the lace colour of each regiment. A few regiments did not have the usual Swedish-pattern cuffs with cuff flaps, instead having Prussian-pattern cuffs, which were round and had both piping and lace loops on the buttonholes in the lace colour of each unit. The skirts of the coat were turned back in order to reveal the colour of the lining, which corresponded to the facing colour. A single shoulder strap, in scarlet red, was worn on the rear of the left shoulder. The coats of grenadiers had distinctive shoulder wings in the lace colour of each regiment. The pockets placed at the sides of the skirts were three-pointed and horizontal; they had white metal or yellow brass buttons and were piped in the facing colour of each unit. The vent of each skirt was also lined in the facing colour and had white metal or yellow brass buttons. Six additional buttons with their lace loops on buttonholes were present at the rear waist, having only a decorative function.

Under the coat, which was the main garment of a British infantryman, a coarse linen shirt was worn. Over the shirt, each soldier wore a single-breasted and collarless waistcoat, which was cut longer than waist-level. This had flapped pockets below the waist at each side of the front. The waistcoat was scarlet red and had ten white metal or yellow brass buttons; it was piped in the lace colour on the front and sometimes could have lace loops on the buttonholes. The breeches worn by each infantryman, made of coarse wool with a flap frontal opening, were dyed in scarlet red or in the facing colour of each regiment. The gaiters, extending above the knee and being worn on all occasions, were designed for strength and ease of marching rather than for elegance. They were closed down the outer seam by a row of buttons, with a garter placed below the knee. The gaiters were made of linen for parade use and of ticking for when on campaign; originally they were white, but over time they became black because it was more serviceable than white and presented a more pleasing appearance. The outfit was completed by simple black shoes. During cold months, the British foot soldiers were not issued greatcoats or cloaks, instead having to simply button-up the frontal lapels of their coats. NCOs were uniformed and equipped quite similarly to their men, but with a distinctive red sash around the waist that had a central band in the facing colour of each regiment. The officers' rank was shown by the silver or golden colour of their lace and by aiguillettes, or shoulder knots – always silver or golden – that were frequently worn on the shoulders. One shoulder knot on the right shoulder identified company officers, while one on each shoulder identified field officers. In addition, each officer wore a crimson red sash made of silk over the right shoulder and a metal gorget, either silver or golden, which was tied around the neck with a silk ribbon in the facing colour of each regiment. The gorget bore the regiment's number for most units, except for the foot guards and for some old regiments that had the privilege of bearing the Royal cypher or a regimental symbol. Officers had black leather boots instead of the usual black shoes. Musicians wore elaborate liveries with decorative stripes in silver or gold and in the facing colour of each regiment, and had shoulder wings like those worn by grenadiers. The musicians' coats could also be ornamented with stripes of cloth (usually having a 'V' shape) that were applied on the sleeves and had the same colour/decorative design as the regiment's lace. The pioneers of each regiment were dressed like the grenadiers, the peculiar elements of their personal equipment being a leather apron and their working tools (the axe and the saw).

The standard personal equipment of a British line infantryman comprised just a few elements, which were quite practical to use. At the rear of the right hip, suspended from a wide light brown (later white) buff-leather belt passing over the left shoulder, a massive black leather ammunition pouch was carried. This had a compartmented cartridge-box on the inside and was wax-polished to give a glossy sheen. A large sword-belt made of light brown (later white) buff-leather was worn around the waist, over the waistcoat and over the belt of the ammunition box; this carried the short sword and the bayonet of each foot soldier. Grenadiers carried a larger black leather pouch instead of the standard ammunition pouch, which was used to transport their hand-grenades, and had a smaller ammunition pouch fixed on the front of their waistbelt. As time passed, each infantryman started to carry a white linen haversack over the right shoulder, near the simple tin canteen that was general issue. By the beginning of the Seven Years' War, a calfskin knapsack with light brown or white slings was worn by each foot soldier, containing his personal equipment and spare clothing. The light companies of the line infantry regiments had black leather equipment instead of the standard white. The main weapon of the infantry officers was a straight-bladed sword, which was carried on a waist-belt that was largely concealed by the waist-sash. The sword knot was silver or golden. Officers could also carry half-pikes or espontoons, while NCOs could have halberds. The standard musket employed by the British infantry was the famous Brown Bess, a flintlock weapon that started to be produced in 1722. In 1736, the original weapon was greatly improved, substituting the iron fittings with brass ones and the wooden ramrod with an iron one. These improvements and a standardization in the productive process led to the birth of the Long Land Pattern Musket, the most common version of the Brown Bess. A shorter version of the weapon, originally designed as a carbine for cavalry use, started to be produced in 1746; known as the Short Land Pattern Musket, this was adopted by the light infantry companies and updated in 1756. The Brown Bess had a triangular-section socket bayonet. The sling of the musket was light brown or white. In addition to his musket, each British foot soldier had a secondary weapon, an infantry short sword with a straight blade and cast brass hilt. The infantry short sword was carried in a leather scabbard that had metal fittings.

The coat worn by the Highland regiments was the same as that of all the other units of the British infantry, except for not having coloured lapels on the front. All the belt equipment of the Highland units was black leather, while the Highlanders wore their ammunition pouch on the belly and not on the back. The Highland regiments wore their traditional Scottish kilts instead of breeches, produced with the distinctive pattern of tartan cloth known as Government's Sett. From a distance, the dark green and dark blue of the tartan looked black, and it was for this reason that the 42nd Regiment of Foot received its nickname of the Black Watch. On the front of their kilts, the Highlanders wore the characteristic sporran pouch and usually carried a *sgian-dubh* (pronounced 'skene doo') single-edged knife. Together with standard black shoes, the Highlanders wore their traditional hose socks that were made with white-and-red tartan for all regiments. Highland officers wore their distinctive sashes over the left shoulder. The peculiarities of the Highlanders included another two elements: the use of the Scottish basket-hilted broadsword (the Claymore) and – only on special occasions – the wearing of the full plaid made of tartan cloth that was worn on the left shoulder. The peculiar elements of the Highlanders' dress described above were already present in the outfit of the Independent Highland Companies, whose uniform was inherited by the 42nd Foot. The soldiers of the Invalid Corps were dressed like the ordinary line infantrymen, having royal blue as their facing colour. Their coats did not have frontal lapels and had an old-fashioned unbuttoned long skirt until 1748. The Fencible units were dressed like the Highland regiments of foot. The independent colonial companies deployed in North America and in the West Indies were dressed exactly like the line infantry regiments. The regiments of Marines raised in 1739 and 1740 wore the same coats as the line infantry, but sometimes with folded collar in the distinctive colour of each unit; in addition, some of them had striped gaiters and all of them wore the black ammunition pouch on the front of the waistbelt. The Marines Corps, created in 1755, was dressed like the grenadiers of the line infantry, with mitre cap, its distinctive facing colour being white. The Marines were always dressed in scarlet red, like the line infantry of the British Army, and were consequently soon given the nickname of Lobsters by the sailors who served with them on the warships of the Royal Navy.

The British cavalry was dressed similarly to the line infantry, with no major differences between the dress of the horse regiments and dragoon regiments. The guard cavalry corps, however, did have some special distinctions. The standard headgear of the British mounted troops was the tricorn, which had a narrow lace on the external edge in white or yellow and a button made of white metal or yellow brass at the left front. The button was placed over a black cockade, which had a black loop for rankers and a golden one for officers, while the lacing of the tricorn was silver or golden for officers. The headgear of the Horse Grenadier Guards and the 2nd Dragoons (the Scots Greys) was the mitre cap, entirely made of cloth and having a tall front mounted on shaped stiffened card; the front was embroidered with the Royal cypher surmounted by a crown and encircled by foliate decorative designs. At the bottom of the front face there was a small red flap embroidered with the motto '*Nec Aspera Terrent*' and with the white horse of Hanover. The main body of the mitre cap was in the distinctive facing colour of each unit, while the various decorations were in their distinctive lace colour (white for both the Horse Grenadier Guards and the 2nd Dragoons). At the top of the headgear was a white woollen tuft with a centre of threads in the distinctive facing colour of each regiment. The rear of the cap had a piece of red cloth stitched to the stiffened front and two pieces of cane used to retain the shape of the headgear. Coloured tape was placed over the sides and back of the cap to conceal the stitching. At the rear of the headgear was a tape in facing colour bearing the number of the unit, a flaming grenade and some other foliate decorative designs. The mitre cap had a strip of regimental lace running around its bottom edge. To prevent the headgear from falling off, it was usually fitted with tapes sewn into the lining and tied under the plait of the hair. The mitre caps of officers were decorated with silver or golden thread. The new light dragoon regiments formed during the Seven Years' War wore distinctive caps made of black leather. These, sometimes visored, usually had a black leather plate on the front (which could be painted in red) and one on the back. The front plate bore the Royal cypher over the number of the regiment. The light dragoon caps could have a rigid crest decorated with a coloured plume and a band of fur or coloured cloth applied around their main body. Each light dragoon corps had its own distinctive model of leather cap and thus many variations existed.

The standard coat worn by British cavalrymen was almost identical to that used by the infantry, except for a few details. It was full-skirted, having tails that extended so far as the knees. Most of the cavalry regiments had coats without frontal lapels, but a few units had coats with lapels that were designed to button across the chest in bad weather. As with the infantry, the frontal lapels were dyed in the distinctive facing colour of each regiment, which was royal blue for the guard cavalry (except the Horse Guards) and all those units that bore the adjective 'Royal' in their official denomination. The colour of the horse soldiers' coats was the universal scarlet red, which was quite costly to produce. The coats were collarless and had round cuffs of the Prussian pattern, with both piping and lace loops on the buttonholes in the lace colour of each unit. The cuffs were dyed in the distinctive facing colour of each regiment. On the front of the coat there were ten buttons, which could be white metal or brass yellow. The ten buttonholes were decorated with lace loops, which were in the distinctive lacing colour of each regiment (white being the most common). The cuffs could have one or more stripes of lace in the distinctive colour of each regiment. Above the cuff, a cuff flap with a variable number of buttons (usually three or five) was visible, which had piping and lace loops of the buttonholes in the lace colour of each regiment. The skirts of the coat were turned back in order to reveal the colour of the lining, which corresponded to the facing colour. A single shoulder strap, in scarlet red, was worn on the rear of the left shoulder. The pockets placed at the sides of the skirts were vertical, with white metal or yellow brass buttons (usually five) and lace loops on the buttonholes. The vent of each skirt was lined in the facing colour and had white metal or yellow brass buttons. Six additional buttons with lace loops on buttonholes were present at the rear waist, having a decorative function. Several horse and dragoon regiments wore white or yellow aiguillettes or shoulder knots on the right shoulder. The lace loops embroidered on the cuff flaps and on the side pockets of several units were V-shaped. Some regiments had small folded collars in their facing colour. The Horse Guards were the only mounted regiment of the British Army to have dark blue coats with red facings, hence their nickname of The Blues. The Life Guards wore an extremely elaborate version of the standard coat, with folded collar piped in gold. All the buttonholes of their dress had golden lace loops; their side pockets were horizontal, their shoulder strap was piped in gold and their tricorn was edged in gold. The cuff flaps were decorated with several stripes of golden lace. Except for their headgear, the Horse Grenadier Guards were uniformed like the line cavalry. Under the coat, which was the main garment of a British cavalryman, a coarse linen shirt was worn. Over the shirt, each soldier wore a single-breasted and collarless waistcoat, which was longer than waist-length. The waistcoat had flapped pockets below the waist at each side of the front, and was white or buff for most of the regiments, but some had it in their facing colour. It was closed by ten white metal or yellow brass buttons. The breeches used by each cavalryman, made of coarse wool, were white or buff for most of the regiments, but some had them in their facing colour. The outfit was completed by tall grenadier boots made of black leather.

NCOs were uniformed and equipped quite similarly to their men, but wore a distinctive red sash around the waist, which had a central band in the facing colour of each regiment. The officers' rank was shown by the silver or golden colour of their lace and by aiguillettes or shoulder knots – always silver or golden – that were frequently worn on the shoulders. One shoulder knot on the right shoulder identified company officers, while knots on each shoulder identified field officers. Each officer also wore a crimson red sash made of silk over the right shoulder and a metal gorget. The latter, silver or golden, was tied around the neck with a silk ribbon in the facing colour of each regiment and bore the regiment's number for most units, except for the guard corps and for some older regiments that had the privilege of bearing the Royal cypher or a regimental symbol. Musicians wore elaborate liveries with decorative stripes in silver or gold and in the facing colour of each regiment, and usually had decorative shoulder wings. The musicians' coats could also be ornamented by stripes of cloth (usually in a 'V' shape) that were applied on the sleeves and had the same colour and decorative design as the regiment's lace. The farrier of each regiment was dressed with a distinctive dark blue coat that had facings in the regimental colour. Being the equivalent of the infantry unit pioneers, the farrier's headgear was a fur cap similar to that worn by the Highland grenadiers. On the front of the fur cap was a red plate bearing a horseshoe symbol. Each farrier was equipped with an axe and a leather apron.

The standard personal equipment of a British cavalryman comprised only a few elements, all of which were practical to use. At the rear of the right hip, suspended from a wide light brown (later white) buff-leather belt passing over the left shoulder, a massive buff (later white) leather ammunition pouch was carried. This had a compartmented cartridge-box on the inside and was wax-polished to give a glossy sheen. A large sword-belt made of light brown (later white) buff-leather was worn around the waist, over the waistcoat, holding the sword of each cavalryman. The musket, which had a light brown (later white) buff-leather sling, was carried behind the right shoulder. The light dragoons carried their carbines suspended on a leather crossbelt that passed over the left shoulder. The standard sword used by the British cavalry, which was not produced according to a precise model but existed in many variations, had a straight blade and a full basket hilt made of brass or steel. The light dragoons were assigned shorter sabres with a curved blade. The first standardized models of British cavalry swords and sabres were introduced only in 1788. Until 1746, the British cavalrymen were armed with the same flintlock musket as the infantry; in that year, the new Short Land Pattern Musket started to be produced and was adopted by all the mounted units. Each cavalryman was also equipped with a couple of flintlock pistols. Dragoons carried bayonets for their muskets, unlike the members of the horse regiments. Light dragoons were assigned short flintlock carbines, which were not manufactured following a standard model until the introduction of the Eliott Carbine in 1773. The shabraque and holster caps of the British cavalry were in the facing colour of each regiment, with external edging in the lace colour of each corps. The rear corners of the shabraque and the holster caps bore the Royal cypher below a crown or regimental symbol.

The Royal Artillery was dressed similarly to the line infantry, but with dark blue coats having red facings. Its complete outfit was as follows: black tricorn with yellow external edging, black cockade with yellow brass button and yellow holder; dark blue collarless coat with red frontal lapels, Swedish-pattern cuffs and turnbacks; yellow piping around the neck, around the lapels and on the front; yellow lace loops on all the buttonholes (including those of the cuff flaps and side pockets); yellow brass buttons (four on the cuff flaps and four on the vertical side pockets); dark blue waistcoat with yellow piping to the front and yellow lace loops on the buttonholes; dark blue breeches and black or white gaiters. The edging and lacing of officers was golden, and their waistcoats and breeches were white or red. Rank was shown by golden aiguillettes or shoulder knots, the crimson red sash made of silk worn over the right shoulder and the golden gorget. Until 1757, the few officers of the Royal Engineers did not have a peculiar uniform and thus were dressed exactly like the line infantry. But from that year it was prescribed that the distinctive facing colour of their scarlet red coats would be black. The auxiliary corps formed to face the Jacobite Rising of 1745 had quite peculiar uniforms. The various regiments raised by the major aristocrats of Great Britain were uniformed like the regulars but with reversed colours: dark blue coats with red facings. This was the case, for example, with the Duke of Kingston's Horse, which was uniformed like a normal mounted unit despite being trained to act as light cavalry. The Loyal Blue Fusiliers, Liverpool Blues, Yorkshire Blues and Yorkshire Hunters were all dressed in dark blue with red facings (having a quite regular appearance). The Edinburgh Regiment and Glasgow Regiment, formed in Scotland, instead wore grey or brown civilian coats together with blue Highland bonnets with a black cockade. The Georgia Rangers, being a mounted infantry corps more than a true cavalry unit, were dressed like the rangers of the Thirteen Colonies: black leather jockey's cap, entirely medium green short-tailed coat with front lapels and Prussian-pattern cuffs of the same colour, medium green waistcoat and breeches, and black leather boots. The Duke of Cumberland's Hussars, consisting of a few Hungarian light cavalrymen who came from Hanover to act as the personal guard of the duke, were dressed in perfect Hungarian fashion as follows: busby made of brown fur with white decorative cords-and-flounders and red bag of cloth on the left side; medium green dolman with white frontal frogging and piping, and red pointed cuffs piped in white; medium green pelisse with brown fur edging and white frontal frogging; red waistcoat with white frontal piping; red trousers with white Hungarian knots embroidered on the front and black leather grenadier boots. The infantrymen of the Dutch expeditionary corps had a black tricorn with white external edging and black cockade, dark blue coat with red frontal lapels and Prussian-pattern cuffs, buff waistcoat and breeches, and black gaiters. Grenadiers wore a black bearskin with red bag of cloth (having a white tassel) on the back. The single Swiss infantry regiment of the Dutch contingent had a slightly different dark blue coat with red folded collar, white lace loops on the buttonholes and without frontal lapels. The few Dutch artillerymen were dressed like the musketeers of the infantry, but with red waistcoat and breeches.

The Hanoverian musketeers were dressed in red uniforms that were quite similar in their cut to those of the Prussian infantry: black tricorn with white edging, black cockade and pompom in regimental colour; red coat without collar and with frontal lapels in regimental colour; Prussian-pattern cuffs and turnbacks, brass buttons, white brandenbourgs (lace loops) on the buttonholes, waistcoat in regimental colours, straw-coloured breeches, white stockings and buff leather equipment. Grenadiers were uniformed like musketeers, but their headgear was a mitre cap entirely made of cloth, with facing-coloured front bearing embroidered decorations and red bag of cloth on the back. The point of the mitre was surmounted by a pompom in regimental colours. The elite Fussgarde had dark blue as its regimental colour, golden brandenbourgs (also on the buttonholes of the waistcoat) and golden piping to facings. The two guard regiments of the Hanoverian cavalry had distinctive red uniforms. The Leib-Regiment had a black tricorn with silver edging and black cockade, red coat without collar but with frontal lapels in dark blue, red Swedish-pattern cuffs, dark blue turnbacks, silver buttons and straw-coloured waistcoat and breeches. The Grenadieren zu Pferde had a mitre cap entirely made of cloth, with black front bearing embroidered decorations and red bag of cloth on the back. The point of the mitre was surmounted by a red pompom. The uniform included a red coat without collar but with frontal lapels in black, black Swedish-pattern cuffs, red turnbacks, golden buttons, golden aiguillette on the right shoulder and straw-coloured waistcoat and breeches.

The Hanoverian cuirassiers, despite their denomination, were not equipped with cuirasses, being dressed more like dragoons. The uniform consisted of the following elements: black tricorn edged in white with black cockade, white coat without frontal lapels and collar, Swedish-pattern cuffs and turnbacks in regimental colour, white metal buttons and straw-coloured waistcoat and breeches. Dragoons had frontal lapels on their coats, in regimental colours. One company in each dragoon regiment, being designated as a mounted grenadier unit, had a mitre cap in white as headgear. The regular Jager Corps was dressed as follows: black tricorn, dark green coat with dark green frontal facings and Swedish-pattern cuffs, white metal buttons, dark green waistcoat and straw-coloured breeches. Foot jagers had black gaiters, while mounted jagers had black leather boots. The grenadiers of Stockhausen's Jagers wore a peculiar dark green mitre cap. Luckner's Hussars were originally dressed with a black tall mirliton cap, dark green dolman with yellow frogging and piping to facings, dark green pelisse with black fur edging and red leggings with yellow Hungarian knots embroidered on the front. This dress, however, was later discontinued since it was too similar to that worn by a French light cavalry unit. Thereafter, the following new uniform was introduced: black busby with red bag of cloth, white dolman with yellow frogging and piping to facings, red pelisse with black fur edging and white leggings with yellow Hungarian knots embroidered on the front. The carabiniers of Freikorps Scheither had a black tricorn with green cockade, white waist-length Kollet coat in the Prussian style with green edging to the front and turnbacks, green Swedish-pattern cuffs, green waistcoat with white edging to the front and straw-coloured breeches. Both the grenadiers and the jagers of the corps wore green coats without frontal lapels but with green turnbacks; the folded collar and Swedish-pattern cuffs were green (with double zig-zag piping in white for grenadiers). The uniform was completed by a straw-coloured waistcoat and breeches. The grenadiers had a brown fur cap as headgear, while the jagers had a standard black tricorn. Each company of grenadiers and jagers included a detachment of six sappers, who wore a mitre cap with a green turban wrapped around its main body.

The artillery of Freikorps Scheither was dressed like the regular gunners of the Hanoverian Army. The Hanoverian regular artillerymen wore a black tricorn edged in yellow, iron grey coats without frontal lapels and collar, red Swedish-pattern cuffs and turnbacks, iron grey waistcoat and straw-coloured breeches. The infantry of Buckenburg wore a black tricorn with white edging and red over white pompom, dark blue coat without frontal lapels but with red facings and turnbacks, and white waistcoat and breeches. The single grenadier company of the infantry regiment had a brass-fronted mitre cap. The jagers wore a black tricorn, dark green coat with yellow folded collar and Swedish-pattern cuffs, no frontal lapels, dark green turnbacks, yellow waistcoat and dark green breeches. The carabiniers had a metal cuirass and helmet painted in black; the latter, curiously, had a band of dark brown fur wrapped around its main body. The outfit was completed by a black coat with red facings and turnbacks, and straw-coloured waistcoat and breeches. The artillerymen wore a black tricorn, iron grey coat without frontal lapels with black cuffs and red turnbacks, white waistcoat and iron grey breeches. Each of the five battalions and five squadrons that made up the Légion Britannique had a distinctive uniform. The 1st Infantry Battalion had a black tricorn with green cockade, light blue coat with yellow frontal lapels and turnbacks, no collar, yellow Swedish-pattern cuffs and yellow waistcoat. The 2nd Infantry Battalion had a black tricorn with green cockade, dark blue coat without frontal lapels and collar, red Swedish-pattern cuffs and turnbacks, and white waistcoat. The 3rd Infantry Battalion wore a black tricorn with green cockade, white coat with orange frontal lapels and turnbacks, no collar, orange Swedish-pattern cuffs and orange waistcoat. The 4th Infantry Battalion had a black tricorn with green cockade, red coat with light blue frontal lapels and turnbacks, no collar, light blue Swedish-pattern cuffs and buff waistcoat. The 5th Infantry Battalion had a black tricorn with green cockade, red coat without frontal lapels and collar, black Swedish-pattern cuffs and white turnbacks and waistcoat. The 1st Dragoon Squadron had a black tricorn with green cockade, light blue coat without frontal lapels and collar, white Swedish-pattern cuffs and turnbacks, yellow aiguillette on the right shoulder, white waistcoat and buff breeches. The 2nd Dragoon Squadron wore a black tricorn with green cockade, dark blue coat without frontal lapels and collar, red Swedish-pattern cuffs and turnbacks, white aiguillette on the right shoulder, white waistcoat and buff breeches. The 3rd Dragoon Squadron had a black tricorn with green cockade, white coat without frontal lapels and collar, orange Swedish-pattern cuffs and turnbacks, yellow aiguillette on the right shoulder, orange waistcoat and buff breeches. The 4th Dragoon Squadron had a black tricorn with green cockade, red coat without frontal lapels and collar, light blue Swedish-pattern cuffs and turnbacks, white aiguillette on the right shoulder, white waistcoat and buff breeches. The 5th Dragoon Squadron had a black tricorn with green cockade, red coat without frontal lapels and collar, black Swedish-pattern cuffs and turnbacks, white aiguillette on the right shoulder, white waistcoat and buff breeches.

The uniform of the Hesse-Kassel infantry was quite similar to that worn by the contemporary Prussian foot regiments: black tricorn with white edging and pompom in regimental colour, dark blue coat with frontal lapels and turnbacks in regimental colour, no collar, and Prussian-pattern cuffs, waistcoat and breeches in regimental colours. Most of the units had white brandenbourgs on the buttonholes, the number, shape and disposition of which distinguished the various regiments. The brandenbourgs of Guard regiments were tasselled. Belt equipment was white leather. Grenadiers had Prussian-style mitre caps with pompom in regimental colour and cloth in regimental colour on the back. The embossed frontal plate was white metal. The two fusilier regiments had Prussian-style mitre caps, without pompom but with brass frontal plate. Before 1760, the horse regiments wore a black tricorn with black cockade and golden edging, white frock coat with folded collar and Swedish-pattern cuffs in regimental colours, golden piping to facings, white breeches and black leather boots. They were then given Prussian-style dress consisting of a black tricorn with black cockade and golden edging, buff-coloured Kollet coat with facings in regimental colour, golden piping to facings, buff-coloured breeches and black leather boots. From 1760, the Hesse-Kassel heavy cavalry was issued with metal cuirasses painted in black. The dragoon regiments were uniformed like those of the Prussian Army: black tricorn with black cockade and white plume having the base in regimental colour, dark blue coat with frontal lapels and turnbacks in regimental colour, no collar, Swedish-pattern cuffs in regimental colour, straw-coloured waistcoat and buff-coloured breeches. In 1760, the colour of the coats was changed from dark blue to light blue. The uniform of the Hesse-Kassel hussars was as follows: brown busby with red bag of cloth, light blue dolman with yellow frogging and red facings, light blue pelisse edged with brown fur and light blue leggings. The jagers wore a black tricorn, dark green coat with red frontal lapels and turnbacks, red folded collar and Swedish-pattern cuffs, dark green waistcoat and breeches. Chasseur Battalion von Rall wore a black tricorn with white edging and green pompom, light blue coat with green frontal lapels and turnbacks, no collar, green Swedishpattern cuffs and green waistcoat and breeches. All the Hesse-Kassel artillerymen were uniformed as follows: black tricorn with white edging and red pompom, dark blue coat with red frontal lapels and turnbacks, red folded collar and Prussian-pattern cuffs, and dark blue waistcoat and breeches. The Hesse-Kassel militiamen wore a black tricorn with white edging, dark blue coat without frontal lapels and collar but with red turnbacks and Swedish-pattern cuffs, and straw-coloured waistcoat and breeches.

The general appearance of the Brunswick infantry was very Prussian, its uniform consisting of the following elements: black tricorn with black cockade and white edging, dark blue coat with frontal lapels and turnbacks in regimental colour, folded collar and Swedish-pattern cuffs in regimental colour, and white waistcoat and breeches. The grenadier companies and units wore a mitre cap which had the cloth on the back in regimental colour, a white metal frontal plate and a pompom in regimental colour. Belt equipment was white for all foot units. Until 1759, the uniform of the Brunswick dragoons was as follows: black tricorn with black cockade, golden scalloped edging and yellow pompom, red coat without frontal lapels, yellow folded collar and Swedish-pattern cuffs, yellow turnbacks and brandenbourgs on the buttonholes, and yellow waistcoat and breeches. In 1759, a new dress, very similar to that of the Prussian cuirassiers, was introduced: black tricorn with black cockade, golden scalloped edging and yellow pompom, buff-coloured Kollet coat with red facings, buff-coloured breeches and black leather boots. The uniform was worn with a metal cuirass painted in black. The hussars' uniform consisted of a tall grey busby with yellow bag of cloth and white plume having a red base, yellow dolman with white frontal frogging and edging to facings, violet collar, violet pelisse with white fur edging and yellow leggings with white Hungarian knots embroidered on the front. The Brunswick jagers wore a black tricorn with green pompom, medium green coat without frontal lapels, red folded collar and turnbacks (straw-coloured for mounted companies), medium green waistcoat and straw-coloured breeches. Light Infantry Battalion von Barner wore a black tricorn edged in white with half-white and half-yellow pompom, dark blue coat without frontal lapels, black folded collar and Swedish-pattern cuffs, red turnbacks and white waistcoat and breeches. The foot grenadiers of the Volontaires Auxiliares de Bronswick wore a mitre cap, light blue coat with green facings, green waistcoat and straw-coloured breeches. The mounted grenadiers were dressed like the foot units but their coats were dark blue instead of light blue. The hussars had a tall black busby with yellow bag of cloth, dark blue dolman with yellow frontal frogging and facings, dark blue pelisse with black fur edging and dark blue leggings with yellow Hungarian knots embroidered on the front. The *Bosniaken* were dressed like those of the Prussian Army, with dark grey kaftan having white trimming and light blue baggy trousers. Their headgear was a red fez with a white turban wrapped around its body. The Brunswick artillerymen were uniformed as follows: black tricorn with yellow edging, dark blue coat without frontal lapels and collar, red Swedish-pattern cuffs and turnbacks, and straw-coloured waistcoat and breeches.

The various regular units raised by the British in the Thirteen Colonies were usually dressed like the rest of the British line infantry; this was the case, for example, with Shirley's Regiment of Foot and Pepperell's Regiment of Foot. Gooch's Regiment of Foot, being a naval infantry unit, had a simplified version of the standard infantry coat that did not have frontal lapels. The independent infantry companies stationed in the Thirteen Colonies were dressed like the British line infantry, with green as their facing colour, until 1760. During that year, the four companies garrisoning New York were assigned a new dress in North American style: black tricorn with white edging and black cockade, dark green short-tailed coat without frontal lapels and with horizontal side pockets, buff breeches and Indian-style dark green leggings. The 80th Foot, being a ranger unit raised for service in the woodlands of North America, wore a peculiar campaign uniform: black leather jockey's cap with a tuft of black wool on top, medium brown short-tailed coat with horizontal side pockets, dark brown frontal lapels and dark brown round cuffs, medium brown waistcoat and breeches, light brown gaiters and black shoes. The first uniform of the Nova Scotia Rangers was quite simple: black leather jockey's cap, light grey short-tailed coat without frontal lapels but with horizontal side pockets, light red waistcoat, light grey breeches and Indian-style brown leggings. In 1761, they adopted the following new dress: black leather jockey's cap, red short-tailed coat with horizontal side pockets, brown frontal lapels and round cuffs, brown waistcoat, buff breeches and black gaiters. The coat was reversible, so it could be worn with reversed colours on campaign (brown with red facings). Rogers' Rangers had a smart campaign uniform that was perfect for fighting in the woods of North America: black leather jockey's cap, dark green short-tailed coat with horizontal side pockets, dark green frontal lapels and round cuffs, dark green waistcoat and breeches, and Indian-style brown leggings. The coat of the unit's officers had silver decorative lace loops on the buttonholes of the coat and waistcoat. On campaign, the coat could be replaced by a colonial hunting shirt, made of deerskin and ornamented with coloured fringes. Personal equipment was reduced to a minimum and generally included a bag of *wampum* in addition to a horn for transporting the black gunpowder. Weaponry comprised a hatchet and a hunting knife in addition to a rifled flintlock musket. For the campaign of 1759–1760 fought against the French in Canada, both the Nova Scotia Rangers and Rogers' Rangers were given a 'temporary' uniform designed to distinguish the ranger companies in British service; this consisted of a blue Highland bonnet with black cockade, black short-tailed coat with horizontal side pockets, medium blue frontal lapels and round cuffs, black waistcoat, buff breeches and Indian-style black leggings. The Queen's Royal American Rangers were uniformed similarly to Rogers' Rangers: black leather jockey's cap with medium green plume and front plate painted in green bearing the inscription '*Per Silvas*' ('through the woods'), medium green short-tailed coat with horizontal side pockets, medium green frontal lapels and round cuffs, yellow lace loops on the buttonholes of the frontal lapels and cuffs, medium green waistcoat with yellow lace loops on the buttonholes, medium green breeches and Indian-style brown leggings. The militias of the Thirteen Colonies usually had no uniforms to speak of, since their members were dressed in their civilian clothes; the Provincials, instead, were uniformed similarly to the British line infantry. In most cases, their coats were dark blue or dark green with red facings, while they could have frontal lapels and lace loops on the buttonholes.

The European infantry of the East India Company were dressed with red coats that were identical to those worn by the contemporary British line infantry, except for being lined with cotton instead of wool. The facing colour used by all units was yellow, while the lace colour was white. The black tricorn, so popular in Europe, was rarely seen in India, frequently being replaced by a broad-brimmed straw hat or a 'solar *topee*'. The latter, egg-shaped and having a short brim, was made of white linen stretched over a rattan framework; that worn by the European units of Madras had a black plume on the front, together with an oval badge of the same colour that was held in place by two crossed bars of rattan. The artillery of the East India Company, consisting of Europeans, was dressed similarly to the European infantry but – like the British Royal Artillery – with dark blue coats having red facings and yellow lace loops (the latter were white for the European infantry of the company). The Indian auxiliary cavalry did not have uniforms to speak of, since they were dressed with their traditional costumes, like the early infantry companies of sepoys raised by the British. However, they gradually received regular uniforms after they were assembled into permanent battalions. All the sepoys wore a short-tailed scarlet red coat with coloured frontal lapels and round cuffs, worn over a plain white waistcoat. The short turnbacks were in the same colour as the frontal lapels. A standing collar and shoulder straps, always in the same colour as the frontal lapels, were later added to the sepoys' coat. Buttonholes could have white or yellow lace loops, while grenadiers had white or yellow shoulder wings. Sometimes the coat could be without frontal lapels. The sepoys usually wore a coloured sash around their waist, which helped to identify the various units, and also had white short trousers, decorated with coloured embroidering on the bottom edge. What distinguished the sepoys of one presidency from those of another was their headgear. The Indian infantrymen from Madras wore a flat and wide-brimmed blue turban having a tassel in contrasting colour; those from Bengal had the sundial turban – black or blue, short-brimmed – whose name derived from the pointed triangular badge it had on the front (bearing the unit number); the sepoys from Bombay wore a tall egg-shaped blue turban, which could have a decorative brass plate on the front for grenadiers. The Bengal foot soldiers gradually replaced their original sundial turbans with new bell-shaped ones that were made of blue cloth stretched over a rattan or bamboo armature, which could be decorated with white or yellow bands of cloth.

Select Bibliography

Barnes, R.M., *A History of the Regiments and Uniforms of the British Army* (Seeley Service, 1950).

Chartrand, R., *British Forces in the West Indies 1793–1815* (Osprey Publishing, 1996).

Chartrand, R., *Canadian Military Heritage: Volume II (1755–1871)* (Art Global, 1995).

Chartrand, R., *Colonial American Troops 1610–1774 (1)* (Osprey Publishing, 2002).

Chartrand, R., *Colonial American Troops 1610–1774 (2)* (Osprey Publishing, 2003).

Chartrand, R., *Colonial American Troops 1610–1774 (3)* (Osprey Publishing, 2003).

Fraser, D., *The Grenadier Guards* (Osprey Publishing, 1978).

Funcken, F. and Funcken, L., *British Infantry Uniforms: from Malborough to Wellington* (Littlehampton Book Services, 1977).

Grant, C., *The Coldstream Guards* (Osprey Publishing, 1971).

Hofschroer, P., *The Hanoverian Army of the Napoleonic Wars* (Osprey Publishing, 1989).

Lawson, C.P., *A History of the Uniforms of the British Army* (Littlehampton Book Services, 1974).

May, R., *The British Army in North America 1775–1783* (Osprey Publishing, 1998).

Reid, S., *18th Century Highlanders* (Osprey Publishing, 1993).

Reid, S., *British Redcoat 1740–1793* (Osprey Publishing, 1996).

Reid, S., *King George's Army 1740–1793 (1)* (Osprey Publishing, 1995).

Reid, S., *King George's Army 1740–1793 (2)* (Osprey Publishing, 1995).

Reid, S., *King George's Army 1740–1793 (3)* (Osprey Publishing, 1996).

Reid, S., *Redcoat Officer 1740–1815* (Osprey Publishing, 2002).

The Company of Military Historians, *Military Uniforms in America: The Era of the American Revolution* (Presidio Press, 1975).

Zaboly, G., *American Colonial Ranger* (Osprey Publishing, 2004).

Index